# MASTER
## YOUR CRAFT

### Strategies for Designing, Making, and Selling Artisan Work

Tien Chiu

Schiffer Publishing Ltd®

4880 Lower Valley Road • Atglen, PA 19310

**Other Schiffer Books on Related Subjects:**

*Bartram's Boxes Remix,* The Center for Art in Wood,
ISBN 978-0-7643-4736-8

*Award-Winning Basket Designs: Techniques and Patterns for All Levels,* Pati English,
ISBN 978-0-7643-4971-3

*Color: Light, Sight, Sense,* Moritz Zwimpfer,
ISBN 978-0-88740-139-8

Designed by Brenda McCallum
Cover design by Brenda McCallum
Type set in DINEngschrift/Times New Roman

Front cover images: *Center*, Hiroshi Ogawa, *Tea Bowl* (Courtesy of Eutectic Gallery). *From top*: Guy Corrie (Photo: Paul J. Smith). Wayne Wichern (Photo: Jason Wells). Tommye McClure Scanlin. Mea Rhee. John Marshall. Peter Danko (Photo: Tim Rice).

Back cover images, left to right: Ellen Wieske, *Garden Necklace* (Photo: Robert Diamante). Paul Marioni, *FLASH* (Photo: Russell Johnson). John Marshall, *View of San Francisco from the North Bay*.

Page 5 image: Peter Danko, *Atmos Rocker* (Photo: Tim Rice).

ISBN: 978-0-7643-5145-7
Printed in the USA

Published by Schiffer Publishing, Ltd.
4880 Lower Valley Road | Atglen, PA 19310
Phone: (610) 593-1777; Fax: (610) 593-2002
E-mail: Info@schifferbooks.com
Web: www.schifferbooks.com

For our complete selection of fine books on this and related subjects, please visit our website at www.schifferbooks.com. You may also write for a free catalog.

Schiffer Publishing's titles are available at special discounts for bulk purchases for sales promotions or premiums. Special editions, including personalized covers, corporate imprints, and excerpts, can be created in large quantities for special needs. For more information, contact the publisher.

We are always looking for people to write books on new and related subjects. If you have an idea for a book, please contact us at proposals@schifferbooks.com.

For Edouard, who read the first 10,000 pages;
for Lieven, who read every draft;
and for Mike, whose love made it possible.

# CONTENTS

# EXERCISES

# FOREWORD

Every successful craftsperson faces challenges in the production of their work. Some master only a few steps toward the production of their artistic vision, while others are proficient at many steps. Few craftspeople, however, master all the skills necessary to sustain themselves as craft professionals—strong design, production, and sales skills. Whether a craftsperson is called an artist, maker, or any other name, success is always defined by three skills: how one designs, builds, and sells artisanal work.

To execute an artistic vision, a craftsperson must know design as well as how to use materials; design is one of the most important factors for success. Whether a craftsperson is engaged in small-batch production or making one-of-a kind objects, the design quality will ultimately determine the success of the object in the marketplace. And the marketplace matters. In the truest sense of the word, a professional craftsperson is an entrepreneur, a person who takes the initiative to develop a business.

Success in the marketplace has implications beyond the individual artist. It is key to the craft field's future and also an important area of work for the American Craft Council. In her opening essay for the 2009 American Craft Council conference catalogue, Dr. Sandra Alfoldy—professor of craft history at Nova Scotia College of Art and Design University and associate curator of fine craft at the Art Gallery of Nova Scotia—summarized the need for success in the marketplace: "The American Craft Council was formed to create improved markets for craftspeople. As much as the Council conferences are about the exchange of ideas, the financial survival of craftspeople is the only way to ensure the development of craft discourse. It is all well and good to pontificate on the deep meaning of the crafts when one is a regularly paid professor, curator, or arts administrator, but it is an entirely different thing when the ability to have time to shape your ideas surrounding craft depends on earning enough through selling your art to cover your expenses." When artists thrive, the whole craft community benefits.

And not only is the financial success of makers imperative to the future of the craft community, it is also vitally important to today's culture at large. Handcrafted objects create real value; people are interested in who made a given object, how it was made, and if it was made locally and responsibly. A well-designed and beautifully handcrafted object, along with the stories of who made it and how, is meaningful to the consumer of the object in ways mass-produced items will never achieve. More importantly, these aspects help consumers express themselves and live fuller lives. This concept is not new; in 1967, Lois Moran—ACC director and later editor in chief of *American Craft* magazine—argued for the value of the handcrafted object. "Man's need and desire for individual expression lead him to seek out objects for his environment which delight and serve him," she wrote. "That the most unique of these objects originate from the hands of skilled craftsmen is as true of the present as it is of the past."

Tien Chiu has written this book to share strategies that have given her and other artists much success. *Master Your Craft* balances encouragement with life lessons from renowned artists such as American Craft Council Fellows Ana Lisa Hedstrom and Paul Marioni. Chiu's expertise guides her readers to consider many beneficial steps to move their careers forward. Unfortunately, there are no guarantees of financial or artistic success for a craftsperson. Chiu's thoughtful strategies, however, give professional artists a structure for success.

Christopher H. Amundsen
Executive Director
American Craft Council

# PREFACE

I'm a maker. I love taking a pile of raw materials and crafting something beautiful and meaningful—well-wrought pieces that will last for decades or more. And I've been quite successful at it. I've been crafting for over 30 years, and have won many awards for my work. My work is well-designed, beautifully constructed, and wholly original.

But I didn't start out making work like that. In fact, I didn't try to design my own pieces until I'd been crafting for almost a decade. It simply didn't occur to me. I wasn't an artist—I had been raised by a pair of scientists and educated at a science and engineering school. Not only did I not consider myself an artist, I didn't even *know* any artists. All of my friends were scientists and engineers. The artists who designed the needlework pieces and knitted shawls that I so faithfully made seemed like mythical beings—people who understood arcane disciplines like art and design and who could distill their wizardly knowledge into recipes to be followed by mortals like, well . . . me.

Eventually, though, I tired of making other people's designs and decided to venture forth on my own. My first attempts were quite traumatic. While I had some construction skills, I didn't know the first thing about the technical aspects of design. So as soon as I stepped off the beaten path, I made tons of mistakes. There was the "quilt of a thousand scraps," for which I accumulated over 200 different fabrics, painstakingly cut pieces to exactly the right size, created an intricate design on a wall of my apartment—and then realized I had cut the fabric pieces off grain, so they wouldn't assemble accurately. (I could have used a muslin foundation to solve the problem, but I didn't know that.) Then there was the attempted bedspread of handspun, naturally-dyed wool yarn, crocheted into little squares—for which I would spin the yarn, of course, and then dye it, using a different natural dye for each square. It was a great idea, but far beyond my attention span, so after a few energetic weeks, it got abandoned.

Fortunately, I'm persistent, and since I learned a little more from each dramatic failure, eventually my designs (and my design skills) improved. But they didn't really take off until I took a serious look at the design and construction process, and applied it to my newly found passion, weaving. The results were astonishing. Within the first two years of taking up weaving, I had won several awards for my work. My third year, I won "Best in Show" at the Conference of Northern California Handweavers for my handwoven, couture-sewn wedding dress. The dress was also published in fiber arts magazines and is now part of the permanent collection at the American Textile History Museum. And in my fourth year of weaving, my Kodachrome Jacket was featured on the front cover of *Handwoven* magazine.

I couldn't believe it. In just a few years, I'd gone from laboring my way through simple designs to creating award-winning show pieces. Yes, I'd studied design. Yes, I'd worked hard on developing technical skills. But the pieces I created were far beyond what I'd thought I could do. Suddenly, I could translate my visions into real, tangible creations. Pure magic.

I could not have done this if I hadn't thought through my creative process. My technical skills were limited, and my design skills still developing. But my approach to design and construction allowed me to create complex and spectacular pieces, without the disasters that plagued my early efforts. That approach was drawn in part from my experience in industry—I had spent nearly two decades as a high-tech project manager specializing in software development.

I knew the industrial processes for creating new products quickly, with minimal effort. By combining the applicable parts of industrial practices with my own experience as a fiber artist, I was able to create my own designs quickly and efficiently. I also learned a lot through the industry practice of reflecting on each of my projects—not just the finished piece, but the process that got me there.

This is the book I wish I'd read when I started designing my own work. I hope that it enables you to create your first pieces without pain, develop your own masterpieces over time, and grow your creative spirit for many years to come.

# ACKNOWLEDGMENTS

"It takes a village to raise a child," they say, and the same was true of writing this book. I would like to thank the many people who made this book possible:

The team at Schiffer Publishing, for doing the heavy lifting during the publication process.

The artists who graciously agreed to be interviewed, and who provided photos of themselves and their work: Ana Lisa Hedstrom, Archie Brennan, Debora Mauser, Ellen Wieske, Guy Corrie, Hiroshi Ogawa, Jane Dunnewold, Joen Wolfrom, John Marshall, Kaffe Fassett, Mea Rhee, Norah Gaughan, Paul Marioni, Peter Danko, Rachel Carren, Roy Underhill, Susan Martin Maffei, Tim McCreight, Tommye Scanlin, Wayne Wichern, and Yvonne Porcella. Special thanks to Hadar Jacobson, Robin Atkins, Claudia Segal, and Janet Dykstra, who do not appear in this book but whose interviews provided valuable background when I was doing my research.

Laura Fry, who transcribed my artist interviews. I could not have done this without her.

The photographers who shot my work for me: Joe Decker and Lieven Leroy.

The people who helped me with the book proposal: Jan Allegretti, my writing coach; Hal Zina Bennett, who provided encouragement and advice; my proposal readers, especially Carla Gladstone, Julie Bracker, Rachael Herron, Bernadette Murphy, and Lieven Leroy; and Susan Wilson, who introduced me to her editor at Schiffer Publishing.

The Pens and Needles writers' group on Ravelry.com, for their support and encouragement throughout the process. I'm looking at you, Larissa Brown (LarissaBrown), Jennifer Runion (Cetacea), Julie Bracker (pixxicat), and Tana Lovett (frogmented). Special thanks to Eleanor Campion (EleanorLM) for giving me the idea of writing a book blog.

The people who helped me find and contact artists to interview: Paul Smith, Janet Schaller, Tim McCreight, Tommye Scanlin, and Joan Phillips, among many others.

Nina Amir, whose book *How to Blog a Book: Write, Publish, and Promote Your Work One Post at a Time* inspired me to get started.

The many beta readers who returned valuable feedback, including Carla Gladstone, Lisa Dusseault, Rachel Gollub, Joseph Beckenbach, Julie Bracker, Bernadette Murphy, and Tana Lovett. Special thanks to my critique partner, Lieven Leroy, who gave feedback on every one of my many drafts.

Finally, the biggest thanks goes to my long-suffering husband, Mike Magin. Without his love and support, this book would not have been possible.

# INTRODUCTION

Designing your own craftwork is a wonderfully exciting activity. You've got a vision. You know what you want to make. You know what it looks like, what it's going to do. It's going to be wonderful. All you have to do is make it. Right?

Alas, no. Designing your own pieces, while exciting, can be frustrating, too. Nothing ever goes quite as expected—you will have setbacks and triumphs, new ideas that insist on being worked in, and problems that may force you to rethink everything about the piece. By the time you finish, what you have may not resemble your original vision. Some people find this so frustrating that they give up. And that's a pity, because with a little attention to the creative process, anyone can design and create original work. But you need to understand how the design process works, and develop your skills in using that process.

This book provides a framework for designing and making original craftwork, and for developing your skills and artistic voice over your entire body of work.

**Chapter 1: What You Need to Start Designing** discusses skills and traits you will need to start creating your own work. **Chapter 2: The Creative Cycle** provides a framework for the creative process. You'll learn how to create original work in short cycles: Designing, constructing a little bit of your design, evaluating what you've built, and then making whatever design changes are needed before building another small portion.

**Chapters 3 through 7** discuss how to get started with the Creative Cycle—finding ideas and brainstorming the first set of designs to work with. They also offer some suggestions for ways to improve the visual and functional design of your piece, and tips on how to make sure it will be practical to construct. **Chapter 8: Constructing Your Piece** addresses strategies for building your piece.

**Chapter 9: Evaluating Your Work-in-Progress** and **Chapter 10: Evolving Your Design** discuss the central steps of the Creative Cycle—evaluating your design, then changing the design to build on its strengths and eliminate the weaknesses that you found in your evaluation.

The remaining chapters will help you develop your skills, your creative voice, and your career (should you want one). **Chapter 11: Celebrations and Contemplations** discusses how to evaluate a project: Examine your process and what you learned as well as your completed piece. **Chapters 12 and 13** offer suggestions on growing your skills and finding your distinctive personal style. And **Chapter 14: Selling Your Work** offers tips to those who want to find sales outlets for their work, and possibly develop it into a career.

You will find this book helpful if you want to:

## IMPROVE YOUR CREATIVITY:

- Discover how to find inspiration from even mundane things
- Learn ways to brainstorm tons of original designs from just a few seed ideas

## TAKE YOUR WORK TO THE NEXT LEVEL:

- Understand how to design something that will be visually effective, useful, and practical to make and/or sell
- Get a framework for evaluating and improving your work, either in a single piece or as a series

## GROW AS AN ARTIST:

- Improve your skills
- Develop your artistic "voice"

## LEARN HOW TO SELL YOUR WORK:

- Price your work effectively
- Understand the two major routes to selling craftwork.
- Assess whether your work is profitable, and whether you are earning a living wage.

*Master Your Craft: Strategies for Designing, Making, and Selling Artisan Work* draws from both my own experience as an award-winning fiber artist and from the experience of the twenty-two master artisans whom I interviewed for this book. Throughout the book, you'll find insights from highly experienced glassworkers, ceramicists, woodworkers, quilters, weavers, metalworkers, and other artisans across a wide range of media. I've also included tips and tricks drawn from my experience in industry—nearly two decades as a high-tech project manager specializing in new product development. The software industry, whose lifeblood is building complex new products at a rapid pace, has developed processes for testing new ideas efficiently and building complicated software without wasting time, money, or effort. Where those processes are applicable to craft, I have brought them in and fused them with more traditional craft methods to help you create better pieces, with less effort.

There is nothing quite like the thrill of creating beautiful, original craftwork. I hope this book helps you savor that thrill—not just once, but for the rest of your days.

# WHAT YOU NEED TO START DESIGNING

Design isn't easy. Many people choose to follow published project instructions because their first efforts at original design looked as lumpy as a child's first efforts.

But don't give up! You wouldn't start a new craft and expect to make masterpieces instantly, and the same can be said for design. Like any other craft, design has its techniques, tools, and ways of thinking, and it takes time and practice to handle them skillfully. With patience and attention to the details in this book, you'll soon be producing work you'll be proud to share.

What do you need to get started? Joy in learning, a willingness to produce imperfect work, faith in yourself, and the persistence to overcome failure.

## JOY IN LEARNING

The desire to explore is the fundamental driver for creative work. Makers want to know "What happens if I try this?" Indulge your curiosity, try that new approach or idea you may have squelched before, and before you know it, you'll be deep in original work.

Use your brain, your body, your senses of sight and sound and everything else—to observe what's happening. Then, take that observation and apply to it to other circumstances in your medium, in your surroundings, in your life. Because that's the joy of being alive, and that's the joy of working in any medium. If it doesn't bring joy into your life, you're in the wrong field.

*John Marshall, surface design artist*

John Marshall. *View of San Francisco from the North Bay*, 2010. Katazome (stencil-applied paste resist) over silk jacquard, natural pigments. 24" x 24".

# WILLINGNESS TO BE IMPERFECT

The second requirement for creating original work is a willingness to make imperfect work. Original work is almost never perfect, because if you're making something wholly new, you're doing something that you've never done before. That means you'll make mistakes. This is true for experts as well as for novices. Trying to avoid those mistakes is futile, and can cripple your creativity. If you are doing creative work, you will make mistakes. So let go of the desire for perfection, and embrace the idea of exploring instead.

Creativity and perfection just don't go hand in hand. If you're going to work on being creative, you have to forget about being perfect.

When you want to do something perfectly, it means that you already know how to do what you're planning on doing. If you're doing something creatively, it usually means that some part of your journey is going to be different. It's something you've never done before.

What gets your soul going is trying the new and fascinating. But you have no idea how it's going to work out, or even if it's going to work out.

*Joen Wolfrom, quilter*

Joen Wolfrom. *Iris Beckoning*, 1996. Quilt sewn from cotton fabrics. 40" × 60". *Photographer: Ken Wagner.*

There's a lot of imperfection in my work! I'm quick and inspirational. I leave a lot of rough corners which I'm rather fond of.

And one fabulous quilt maker—really, really good—told me, "If I make something for a competition, it's not an enjoyable process. I am sweating through the whole thing, worrying about every little stitch."

So I just don't worry about imperfections.

*Kaffe Fassett, knitter, needlepoint designer, and quilter*

---

# FAITH IN YOURSELF

The third thing you need to design your own work is faith in yourself.

Many beginning (and not-so-beginning) crafters are terrified of taking a close look at their work, or of showing it to others, because they're excruciatingly aware of all their mistakes, and are afraid of being told their work is no good, that they're not a "real" artist. They're afraid that they have no talent and are doomed to mediocrity.

This fear, while understandable, is hogwash. Anyone who creates is doing something artistic—even if the piece is as primitive as a child's first finger painting. And talent is just an aptitude for learning. It doesn't have anything to do with whether a piece is good or bad. You do not need talent to produce good work. What you need is *skill*, and skills need to be developed. In short, your early work will almost certainly be poor, especially compared to your later work (or to experts who have been doing this for decades). So your initial work won't be museum quality. This has nothing to do with talent and nothing to do with being an artist; it's just the way the world works.

Because you haven't developed design skills yet, you'll make mistakes in your early work. So you need to have the courage to fail, to fall down, and then to get back up and try again. Keep faith. Failure is an essential part of the road to mastery.

You need to be a risk taker. But you can learn to be a risk taker.

We have this idea that it's going to be perfect. That we are going to do something and it's going to be wonderful. We don't realize that we have to do things in baby steps.

We need to give ourselves permission to go through this process. It's like riding a bicycle. I can't believe how many scraped knees I had. But I wanted to be able to ride so badly that I got up and did it. So does every child. I don't know of any child who doesn't know how to ride a bicycle if they've been given a bicycle.

It's the same thing. But you have to have an environment that is positive and you have to be around people who promote your courage.

*Joen Wolfrom, quilter*

Debora Mauser. *Untitled*, 2014. Copper, brass, and enamel. 2" × 3". *Photographer: Debora Mauser.*

Lack of confidence is the biggest problem my students have. If it's a new technique, they're always afraid they won't live up to their own expectations. I try to tell them that when we're working on something new, there are no expectations. That you have to realize that if it's a new technique, you won't be perfect. You have to practice, practice, practice. I try to open up their minds to the idea that they can learn something if they are willing to make mistakes as they go.

*Debora Mauser, metalworker*

# PERSISTENCE

It takes time to master the skills to design and execute original work. The joys of creation are inevitably mixed with the frustration of trying—and failing—to make something work. If you have the persistence to work through the early failures, you'll reap the rewards further down the road.

If students are struggling, and saying "I can't do this," I say, "Come on, you want to pick up the bow and be able to play [a violin] first time out? With two hours of instruction?" You can't play a musical instrument like that, and it's the same thing with woodworking. It's hard.

*Roy Underhill, woodworker*

I'm pretty big on trial and error. I think that many, many creative ideas come from failing. We have to be willing to fail.

*Jane Dunnewold,*
*surface design artist*

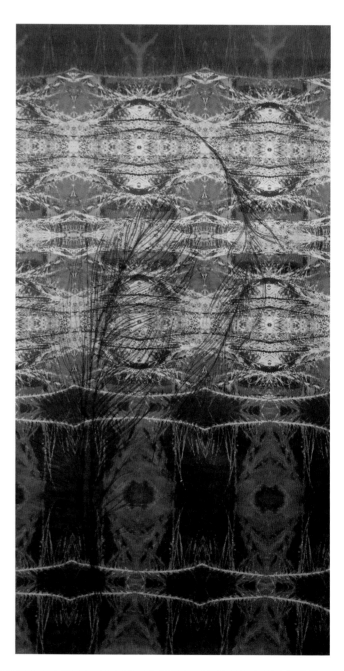

Jane Dunnewold. *Feather Study 1*, 2013. Digitally printed fabric from a photo of a feather as viewed under a microsope, assembled and backed. Machine quilted. 44" × 70".
*Photographer: Jane Dunnewold.*

# SKILLS

In order to design and create your own work, you'll also need to develop four skills:

*Functional design skills* help you create an item that will serve its purpose. Functional design lets you translate a user's needs into a design for an object that fulfills those needs. Chapter 4, "Functional Design," discusses ways to think about the person who will use your product, understand what will make your piece helpful to that person, and design your piece to fill the user's functional needs.

*Visual design skills* are about appearance. Does your piece coordinate with its surroundings? Think about how the viewer's eye moves through your piece, and what it will see on its way. Did your viewer see the piece as you intended? Chapter 5, "Visual Design," describes some ways to think about visual design.

*Technical design skills* translate your design into a blueprint for construction. While the exact details of technical design vary from medium to medium, you can find some general considerations for technical design in chapter 7, "Practical Considerations," and in chapter 8, "Constructing Your Piece."

Finally, *construction skills* are the manual skills needed to fashion a piece. Because every medium requires different skills and techniques, this book does not cover specific construction skills. However, construction strategies are discussed in chapter 8, "Constructing Your Piece," and you can find general suggestions for developing construction skills in chapter 12, "Sharpening Your Skills."

The good news is that you don't need to be an expert in functional design, visual design, technical design, or construction to design and make original work. Think of each of these skills as a process, not a prerequisite. As your mastery improves, so will the quality of your finished pieces. So don't worry if you believe some of your skills are lacking—and certainly don't let it hold you back. Just start in. Consider your first projects learning exercises. Let go of wanting perfection, and focus on enjoying and exploring the medium instead. If you enjoy what you're doing, you'll develop the skills you need.

I asked him how he came to be a painter. He said, "I liked the smell of the paint."

*Annie Dillard, writer,* The Writing Life[1]

# THE CREATIVE CYCLE

Many people think of creating a piece as a linear process—design the piece and then make it, exactly as originally designed. Using a linear process is sometimes possible, especially in simpler projects. But complex, original designs generally follow a more evolutionary path. They change throughout the process as you get new ideas, correct mistakes, and work around flaws in your material. In fact, the finished piece may not resemble the original idea in the least. Change is inevitable—and the tighter you cling to the idea of executing your original vision, the more frustrated you will get.

But there's a better way. Instead of resisting the idea of changing your design, embrace change. In fact, build your entire creative process around it! Allow the piece to evolve and improve throughout the design and construction of the piece. Use construction strategies that allow ample room for last-minute decisions. Evaluate your piece after each addition to see if the design is working.

Surprisingly, the original concept for a piece, while alluring, is rarely the strongest design. That's partly because the concept is usually pretty vague compared to the details of your finished piece. But it's also because you learn more about the piece as you make it—as you refine the design and start bringing it to life, you examine every aspect closely, in far more detail than your original sketch did. Weak spots in the original design become obvious, and ideas for strengthening the better parts will crop up. So executing the project exactly as conceived is not only impossible, it's undesirable. Evolving your work produces stronger pieces.

So how do you build a creative process around change? It's pretty simple. You come up with a design for a piece. Then you create just enough of the piece to test that design. Then you evaluate what you have made, identify what you would like to change, and alter the design to accommodate the change. Keep doing this until you arrive at a result you like. Then, celebrate your finished piece. This cycle—design, create, evaluate, change—is the Creative Cycle.

The Creative Cycle sounds laborious, but it isn't. Reflecting often, instead of a few times, allows you to make small, quick changes rather than big, time-consuming ones. It also lets you spot opportunities for improvement early, when they are still easy to take advantage of. By designing your pieces for change, you can produce much stronger pieces with much less fuss than if you were trying to execute a single monolithic vision.

Let's take a closer look at the Creative Cycle.

FIGURE 2-1. The Creative Cycle.

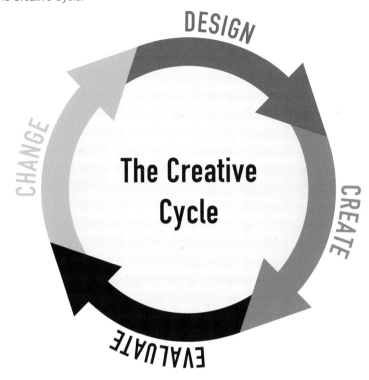

## THE CREATIVE CYCLE DEFINED

The first step in the Creative Cycle is to **Design** the piece. For complex projects, that may mean developing a vague sketch laying out the vision for the piece. For simpler projects, it may encompass a blueprint for the entire piece.

The next step in the creative cycle is to **Create**. Start making whatever you've designed. Not the entire project—just the rough outline. Forget the details; make just enough to evaluate the major elements of the overall design.

Once you've created enough to test your design, step back and **Evaluate** what you've done. Start by concentrating on what you like. What aspects are working for you? How can you build on them? While it is natural to focus on the things you *don't* like, you will get a better piece if you build on what is working rather than subtract everything that doesn't work. (You will also dread evaluating less if you aren't tearing your work to pieces.)

The fourth step in the Creative Cycle is to **Change** the design based on what you've discovered in your evaluation. Think of ways to strengthen the elements you like. Then, think about how you might eliminate the weak points.

Finally, return to the Design phase. Do your changes work well with the rest of the design? If not, rework the design as needed, and Create a new test of that design. Then evaluate your change. If you're happy with it, continue developing your piece. If you're not, keep going through the Creative Cycle until you're satisfied with your changes.

Guy Corrie. *Manhattan Line*, 1989. Blown glass.
*Photographer: Guy Corrie.*

[The design] comes off a napkin, to the blowing floor. We do some offhand prototypes. We like the look and feel of the product, so we do limited production runs. Then we go back and evaluate. How does it feel? How does it look? Does the stem need to be longer? Is the foot too small? There's a lot of give and take until you finally feel, "Well, this is accomplished, and I think it's elegant, and I think we can bring in a line."

*Guy Corrie, glassblower*

# EXAMPLE—*AUTUMN SPLENDOR*

Here's an example, drawn from the construction of my garment *Autumn Splendor*.

In the first Design phase, I started with a vision: falling autumn leaves drifting to the ground. Using some of the methods you will find in chapter 6, "Getting Started," I brainstormed ideas for a while, finally making a simple sketch (fig. 2-2)—a coat in autumn colors with an asymmetric collar and a pointed shape on the back.

FIGURE 2-2. Tien Chiu. Preliminary sketch for *Autumn Splendor*, 2012.

You'll notice that my drawing skills are pretty limited. But that's okay—it doesn't need to be a fancy sketch, or an elaborate computer mockup. It's just something to get us started.

The next step in the cycle is to Create. I decided that I should test the garment design first—would the shape and lines of the garment work? I drafted a sewing pattern and stitched up a muslin (a mockup in cheap fabric) so I could get feedback on the design. Since my most pressing design question was whether the lines of the garment would work, I simplified the design to make it easier to construct. Instead of the gradually changing shades, I used just two contrasting colors. The result was the muslin in figure 2-3.

FIGURE 2-3. Tien Chiu. First muslin for *Autumn Splendor*. *Photographer: Lieven Leroy.*

While the mockup I'd Created was still quite rough, it was enough to judge the design. So I went on to Evaluate the muslin. Following the guidelines in chapter 9, "Evaluating Your Work-in-Progress," I started by focusing on the aspects I really liked, so I could build on those rather than dwelling on negatives.

In the case of this muslin, I liked having one dark side and one light side, and I liked the asymmetry in the garment. I also liked the sense of movement generated by the diagonal lines. I decided to build on those three ideas in the next version.

What aspects wasn't I crazy about? The sharp point in both front and back, as the diagonal line reversed. That didn't feel like a drifting leaf to me.

Next, I began Changing the design to incorporate what I'd learned in my assessment. I decided to keep the dark/light contrast between the two sides of the garment, and emphasize the movement by changing the sharp point to sweeping curves. I wanted to increase the asymmetry, so I would make the collar longer. These changes would add drama to the garment, better capturing the swooping feel of leaves blowing in the wind.

Having made my changes, I started the Creative Cycle again. This time, after Designing with some simple sketches, I decided it would be easier to Create my mockup in Photoshop. So I tinkered with some photos of my intended cloth until I arrived at the mockup in figure 2-4:

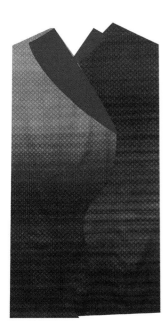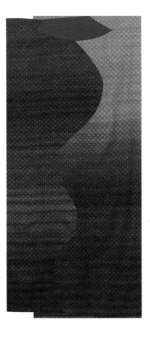

FIGURE 2-4.
Tien Chiu. Photoshop mockup
for *Autumn Splendor*.

This mockup, while quite rough, was enough to let me Evaluate the design. I liked the more dramatic collar and decided to build it further. And I liked the swoopiness of the lines but felt they needed to be more dramatic. So I chose those aspects to Change and started the cycle again. This time I Designed a garment with more movement, Creating the more detailed mockup in figure 2-5.

FIGURE 2-5.
Tien Chiu. Second Photoshop mockup
for *Autumn Splendor*.

When I Evaluated it, this design had great potential—the autumnal colors set the mood beautifully, and the lines resembled the drift of a leaf. No Changes needed. Now I felt that the garment was ready for me to Create another muslin (fig. 2-6).

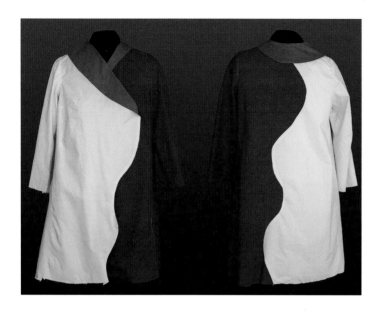

FIGURE 2-6.
Tien Chiu. Second muslin for
*Autumn Splendor*.
*Photographer: Lieven Leroy.*

The lines of the garment still didn't satisfy me—I wanted more dramatic curves. So I continued to Design, Create, Evaluate, and Change over numerous muslins, adjusting the lines each time, until I arrived at a design I liked (fig. 2-7).

FIGURE 2-7.
Tien Chiu. Final muslin for
*Autumn Splendor*.
*Photographer: Lieven Leroy.*

This design finally felt right to me, and I used it in the finished piece (fig. 2-8).

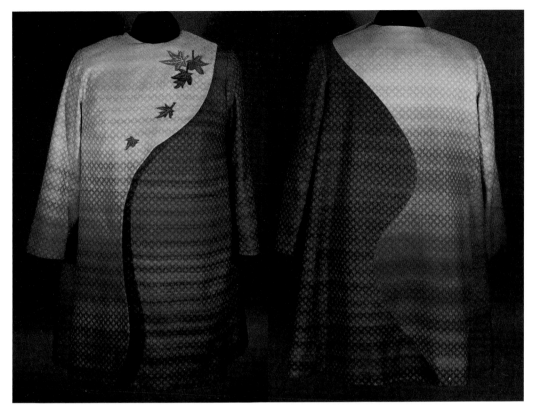

FIGURE 2-8. Tien Chiu. *Autumn Splendor,* 2012. Handwoven swing coat in wool and silk, size 12. *Photographer: Joe Decker.*

You'll notice that the finished garment bears almost no resemblance to the original sketch. But that's okay. Iterating on the Creative Cycle helped me create a garment with far more sophisticated lines and stronger design than if I had tried to design the entire garment at the beginning.

## MISTAKES ARE INEVITABLE

Why would you want to make multiple versions of a design, iterating over and over until you're satisfied? Isn't it more efficient to make one perfect design?

Theoretically, yes. But reality is different. "Get it right the first time" rarely happens when you are making original work, because making something new means you are on unfamiliar ground. So you will make mistakes—lots of them. The key is not to avoid mistakes, but to make sure they don't derail your work. You are not aiming for *no* mistakes, but for faster, cheaper ones. The Creative Cycle lets you design and build in small parts, recognizing your mistakes quickly and fixing them before proceeding.

# USING THE CREATIVE CYCLE FOR
# SMALL CHANGES

The Creative Cycle doesn't just apply to full projects. You can use the Creative Cycle to test out any aspect of your design, no matter how small. Remember, the essential parts of the cycle are: 1) coming up with an idea, 2) building just enough of the idea to be able to see if it works, 3) evaluating the idea, and then 4) changing whatever is needed. Sometimes that means throwing away the idea and trying another, sometimes it just means altering things slightly. The process can be quick or slow, depending on how much needs to be built to see whether your idea works. But in general, aim for the quickest and least expensive way to get your design idea tested.

# MAKING YOUR EXPERIMENTS CHEAPER

Here are some ideas for making the Creative Cycle faster and more efficient:

Start with a sketch. Sketches take just a few minutes and are an easy way to evaluate an initial design concept. Don't feel self-conscious about your drawing skills: you are not trying to be the next Picasso. Nor do you have to show your sketch to anyone else, ever. Instead, you are doodling an idea onto paper to see if it works. Feel free to photocopy or trace parts of your design if that makes it easier.

A computer mockup may also prove valuable, depending on how skilled you are with computer drawing programs. (Some people prefer pencil and paper, and some prefer computers. Some like collage, or watercolor paints. There are no wrong tools in design—if it works for you, it's the right approach.) You can also start with a quick sketch on paper or on a tablet and then move into Adobe Photoshop or Illustrator. These programs allow you to cut and paste parts of a design, create many variations to compare, and quickly import patterns from photos.

Once you're done making mockups on paper and on screen, build a small prototype with cheap materials. Some people feel that samples are a waste, but they're not. They are a way to manage risk. When you make a sample, you are investing some time, effort, and materials to answer a design question that may be critical later in the piece. Is it worthwhile? It depends on the cost of getting your design question wrong. If you've invested in costly materials or have put a lot of time into the project already, mistakes can be expensive and a sample is probably worthwhile. But if there's little or no cost to being wrong, and sampling is expensive or time-consuming, don't sample—you aren't gaining anything by it.

As you progress through the design and construction of the piece, your questions will become more detailed and harder to test cheaply. That's normal. Keep going, but evaluate carefully whether each new sample or prototype is worthwhile.

# APPLYING THE CREATIVE CYCLE ACROSS
# MULTIPLE PIECES

The Creative Cycle doesn't just apply within a single piece. Working in series allows you to apply the Creative Cycle across multiple pieces. Take the strongest points from the previous project and build on them, eliminating the weaker points. You will often find that the final piece in the series comes out much stronger than the first.

Here's an example, from a series of shawls I wove in gradually changing colors.

I started by designing a shawl that shaded gradually from red to gold and back again, patterned with solid black. Here is a photo of my *Black Fire* shawl (fig. 2-9).

FIGURE 2-9.
Tien Chiu. *Black Fire*, 2007. Handwoven shawl in hand-dyed silk thread. 22" × 72". *Photographer: Lieven Leroy.*

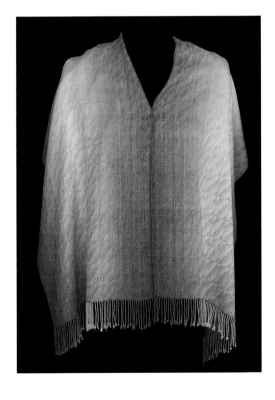

On Evaluating the shawl, I loved the color gradations and the fiery colors. I wanted more bright hues, and more color shifts. I also felt that the shawl could use more variation from one end to the other, so I decided to Change to gradated colors in both directions. Then, I Designed and Created *Liquid Fire* (fig. 2-10).

I felt *Liquid Fire* was stronger than *Black Fire*. But I wasn't quite satisfied. While I loved the color changes, in the spots where similar colors crossed, the woven pattern disappeared. And I felt there could be more variation in the pattern.

FIGURE 2-10.
Tien Chiu. *Liquid Fire*, 2007. Handwoven shawl in hand-dyed silk thread. 22" × 72". *Photographer: Lieven Leroy.*

Back to the Change step. I decided to alter two aspects of the design. First, I made the woven pattern more complex. Then, I changed the colors so the gradually changing weft colors would contrast strongly with the warp colors. I Created a mockup in Photoshop (fig. 2-11), which seemed promising.

FIGURE 2-11. Tien Chiu. Photoshop mockup of *Ocean Sunset* shawl.

On Evaluating, I decided I could use this design without Changes. So I Created the next shawl in the series, *Ocean Sunset.* The resulting piece had the beautiful colored pattern I'd wanted, as you can see in figure 2-12.

FIGURE 2-12.
Tien Chiu. *Ocean Sunset*, 2008. Handwoven shawl in hand-dyed silk thread. 22" × 72".
*Photographer: Joe Decker.*

However, when I put it on, prominent yellow bars appeared, right across my bust line (fig. 2-13). That look was a little too racy for me.

FIGURE 2-13.
Tien Chiu. *Ocean Sunset*, 2008. Handwoven shawl in hand-dyed silk thread. 22" × 72". *Photographer: Lieven Leroy.*

Next I Designed and Created *Ocean Sunset II* (fig. 2-14), with colors that gradually changed from yellow to red and back again over the length of the piece. I had now solved the problem of the prominent bars, but on Evaluating, I decided that while I liked the lengthwise and crosswise color changes, I didn't like the "busy" pattern or the lemon yellow tint at the ends of the shawl.

FIGURE 2-14.
Tien Chiu. *Ocean Sunset II*, 2008. Handwoven shawl in hand-dyed silk thread. 22" × 72". *Photographer: Lieven Leroy.*

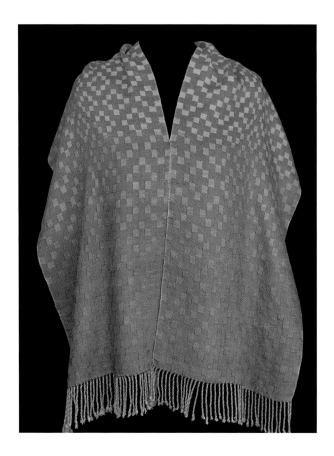

FIGURE 2-15.
Tien Chiu. *Doubleweave Delight*, 2010.
Handwoven shawl in hand-dyed silk
and cashmere thread. 22" × 72".
*Photographer: Lieven Leroy.*

After some thought, I decided to build on the double color gradation, which I liked, and to simplify the pattern. I Designed a new shawl, and Created *Doubleweave Delight* (fig. 2-15).

This piece finally satisfied me, and I moved on to other themes.

While each of these pieces was designed and executed as a single piece, working in series allowed me to develop and explore more designs over a collection of related shawls. While not all the designs were successful, they gradually improved to create a much more sophisticated design than the original piece.

# FINDING INSPIRATION

To start the Creative Cycle, you need an idea, especially since projects rarely spring from nothingness. Usually the starting point is a technique, some materials, a found object, or an abstract idea. Or it could be a piece of your own work or someone else's. Inspiration can come from many places.

## FINDING IDEAS AND INSPIRATION

Finding inspiration is mostly a matter of observation. Look closely at the world around you. Does something look interesting? Snap a picture of it. Keep an eye out for interesting artists, photos, and concepts. Use them in your work.

Jane Dunnewold. *Étude #24: Number 5: Choir*, 2011. Rice paper, felt, pattern paper, sand. 9.5" × 32". *Photographer: Jane Dunnewold.*

Ideas spring up from all kinds of things. I get ideas from looking at things around me. I did a whole series in 2005 that was about boundaries, because I looked out the window and the birds outside were jumping around on the wire. I noticed that when one bird sat down, all the other birds moved over. So I thought "That's an interesting boundary thing." They each had their little six inches between them. And that turned into an exploration—kind of a scavenger hunt approach—discovering other elements that might work with that theme.

　　Another time I was on a flight somewhere and I was looking at the Sky Mall catalog. They had a digital microscope. So I came home, found it somewhere else at half the cost, and bought it. Then I used it to take photographs of things like little bits of feather, and mushroom caps and spider webs. Then I could load them into Spoonflower [a fabric printing service] and create repeating patterns on yardage.

*Jane Dunnewold, surface design artist*

I have a small inspiration book. It has color swatches in there, textures. It could be a piece of material or a leaf that I picked up when I was walking—anything that makes me smile, makes me happy.

That can be an inspiration.

I go back to it when I need to get inspired. I have another book that I actually draw in, that has some shapes and ideas in it. My inspiration book isn't my sketch book.

I use Pinterest [an online photo-collecting service that allows you to share collections of photos with others]. I think the whole world does Pinterest. I have a board that says "Jewelry That Inspires Me." I hardly ever go back to look at it. But when I see something I like, I pin it. So it's there if I want to go back and look.

Same thing with recipes. Anything that looks exciting or interesting. You can use your electronics, social media, Pinterest, whatever, to pin it, then go back and look. And if you do it long enough you'll start seeing the common themes.

For me it's usually texture in the jewelry. In recipes it's usually sweet stuff. I love cakes and cookies.

There's almost always a common theme if people will look at it from that viewpoint. Why did I like all of these? That can start to open up your view of how to move forward in your own work.

*Debora Mauser, metalworker*

Many artists have inspiration notebooks, where they stash photos, web pages, or materials away for future reference.

You don't have to limit yourself to your inspiration book, either. Materials can be a great source of inspiration. Just pick something out of your stash and play with it.

I fall in love with materials. It happens when I appreciate its aesthetic sensibility and I think I can create something with it nobody else has done before. The idea of experimenting with new material excites me.

For years, I've designed molded plywood furniture; I love the process. I loved it because I thought it was mysterious how wood could be shaped like that. I loved its potential to create lyrical and expressive lines. I thought that the craft of molding plywood was underexplored as a medium. It still is.

*Peter Danko, furniture designer*

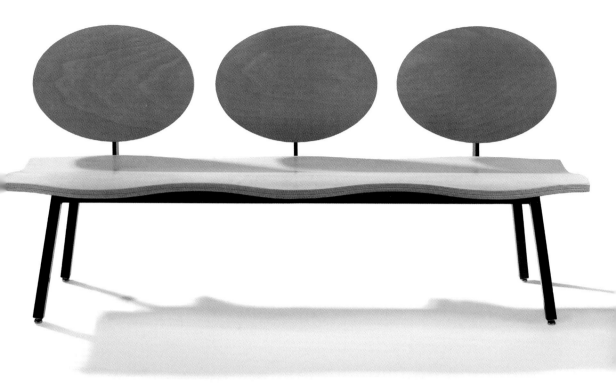

Peter Danko. *Zinnia Bench*, 2001. Steel, maple molded plywood: 72" × 34" × 28". *Photographer: Andy Franck.*

Objects can be a source of inspiration as well. For a weaver, the soft touch of a blue jay feather might inspire cloth as light and soft as that feather. A jeweler working in enamel might find the bars of blue, white, and charcoal gray compelling, and devise a brooch in that palette.

I'm often inspired by things that are completely unrelated to my media. And it could be a word. It could be some other kind of three-dimensional form in another medium. It might be a basket. It might be clay. It could be just a natural form. I did some work that was inspired by termite mounds.

*Andrea Graham, felter*

Ideas can also come out of exploring techniques, especially for new artisans. Pick a technique and just dive in. See how far you can stretch it. Technique-based samples can easily lead into exciting new work.

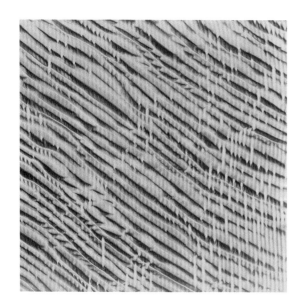

One of my techniques is arashi shibori, wrapping the fabric around a pole [and then dyeing it]. So I'll say okay, it doesn't matter what it is but I'll do something on the pole for an hour. If I keep doing it, something comes from it.

*Ana Lisa Hedstrom, surface design artist*

Arashi shibori fabric by Ana Lisa Hedstrom. *Photographer: Don Tuttle.*

Previous projects provide another wellspring of ideas. Many artisans work in series, producing a group of pieces around a theme, each project yielding ideas for the next project. And ideas often come from working.

And, finally, many pieces start out as abstract concepts. Ideas like beauty, freedom, or death have inspired artists—and artisans– for millennia.

I did a series about Muhammad Ali. I think there were about twelve pieces [in the series]. I wove each piece in a totally different way. Eight of them were from the same press photograph that was a half column wide in the newspaper. It was an inch and a quarter by three quarters of an inch.

I reproduced the light and shades of the image. They all looked exactly like Muhammad Ali, but I developed different techniques to get the whole series.

And that really explains a way [of working]. It explains the whole journey of trying this way, trying that way . . . no, that won't work . . . what would happen if I tried this? That, to me, is the way an artist should work.

*Archie Brennan, tapestry weaver*

I think that an interesting thing happens over a series. At least for me, the first one or two pieces in the series are relatively busy—I'm getting a whole lot of ideas out there all at once. And then the longer I'm willing to stick with the idea and work with it, the more refined and distilled it becomes.

It could go from a piece that actually had a lot of recognizable, figurative imagery on it in the first two or three permutations, but by the time I got to the ninth and tenth pieces, it was just a color field. I think it's almost like settling. I'm driven by a book called the Tao Te Ching, and it says, "Can you be patient enough to allow the mud to settle, to allow the water to clear?" I'm paraphrasing that verse, but that's the idea. And I think that is sort of what happens. At the beginning all the ideas are whipped up and it's exciting to think about and the images are flowing like crazy and then you're figuring out how to get those all down on the two dimensional surface, or in a three-dimensional form, or whatever form your work takes.

And then the more you work with the ideas, the more focused you become on the essence of the idea and then the work simplifies.

And I don't think that one piece is better than another, but they are different.

*Jane Dunnewold, surface design artist*

I've been fortunate enough to go [on retreat] to the Lillian E. Smith Center for about five years. At the Center, there's an old chimney ruin that was part of a larger building on the property at one point. Lillian Smith loved that chimney ruin. When she passed away, one of her requests was that she be buried beside the chimney ruin.

So her grave is there. The only evidence of the grave is a bronze marker with a quote from one of her writings. The quote says, "Death can kill a man; that is all it can do to him; it cannot end his life, because of memory."

Every day I'm on retreat at the Center, I go on a walk. I start it by walking down to the old chimney ruin, looking at Lillian Smith's marker and reading that quote. Last summer I decided to make a tapestry of an enlarged area of the back side of the chimney. So that's how the Stones tapestry began—being in retreat at the Center, thinking about Lillian Smith's quote, and especially the last part of it, "because of memory."

I was thinking about stones and how they hold the memory of our lives in a lot of ways. Even when man puts them together and stacks them up and makes a chimney out of them, or makes a wall out of stones, those stones hold memories that are way beyond our imagining, our understanding. And yet, we, in our finite time, do have memory. We hold the memories of those people who have been important to us, for as long as we are alive.

So that was the basis for the stones tapestry. The title is *Because of Memory*.

*Tommye Scanlin, tapestry weaver*

Lillian E. Smith grave marker, Lillian E. Smith Center, Clayton, GA. *Photographer: Tommye Scanlin.*

Chimney ruin, Lillian E. Smith Center, Clayton, GA. *Photographer: Tommye Scanlin.*

Stones from the back of the chimney ruin, Lillian E. Smith Center, Clayton, GA. *Photographer: Tommye Scanlin.*

Tommye Scanlin. *Because of Memory*, 2014. Handwoven tapestry in wool, cotton. 62" × 59". *©Tim Barnwell Photography*

Finding inspiration is often simply looking closely at something, finding something intriguing about it, and imagining ways to turn that interesting thing into a new piece.

## EXERCISE 1: LEARNING TO SEE

1. Pick an object—something random from around the house or yard, preferably something three-dimensional. It can be interesting to try this exercise even with objects that don't inspire you.

2. Jot down in your notebook your initial reactions to the object—the first few things that strike you. Don't put a lot of effort into it; you're just capturing thoughts as they fly by.

3. Now, look at the shape of the object—not just the whole item, but its parts as well. Does it have interesting curves or jagged edges? Is it long, thin, and delicate, or compact and solid? How does the eye travel through the shape? Write down whatever strikes you as interesting, even if it's not immediately obvious how you would use it in your work. Sketch it or take a photo to illustrate what you are looking at.

4. Now, think about the colors in the object. Are they bright? Dull? Do they have sharp contrasts, or are they mostly similar? What mood do they give the object? What is your off-the-cuff response to the color scheme? Take notes on the colors and your reactions to them. How would you change the color scheme, if you were to change it?

5. Look at the textures in the object. Is it smooth? Rough? Delicately feathered, or solid? Is it all one texture, or is there textural contrast between the parts? Does it have visual patterning, like a tabby cat's stripes? Write down your observations about textures and patterns, along with ideas for further play.

6. Are there any interesting lines in the object? Follow the edges of the object with your fingers (or eyes). What is it about them that draws your attention? What about lines that aren't on edges? Could some of these lines be incorporated into your work? Sketch any interesting lines in your notebook, or trace them on a photograph of the piece.

7. What function, if any, does the object have? What is it intended to do? Are there other things you could use it for? Write down ideas for repurposing the object. Do these repurposed functions spawn ideas for new projects?

8. Finally, free associate on the object. Does it suggest any other objects, themes, ideas, or even projects? Write down the first ten or twenty things that come to mind.

9. Once you've finished, look through your notes and pick out the most interesting ideas. Highlight them in the notebook, or capture them on a separate page. These are grist for your design mill. Let them inspire you to scribble down some thoughts for pieces that might be interesting to make.

If this all seems a bit abstract to you, don't get discouraged. Here's an example of the exercise, done with an object that's so mundane you'd never expect it to be a treasure-trove of ideas.

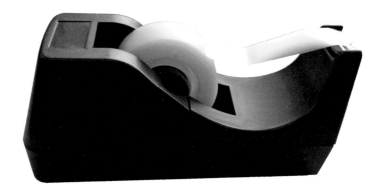

# EXAMPLE: TAPE DISPENSER

## Initial reaction:
It strikes me as mass-produced, modern, sternly utilitiarian, monochromatic—functional but not pretty, or even very interesting.

## Shape:
The shape is more interesting than I thought at first glance. There is an intriguing curve in the black body as you move from the tape-holder portion to the tape-cutting part. Moreover, there are interesting shapes inside the dispenser: the black circle of the widget that holds the tape, the white circles of the tape roll, and the slot the tape roll fits into. The end of the tape makes an interesting negative shape—the curve of the tape dispenser with the curve of the tape roll, coming to an abrupt straight line with the tape. The mostly-curved line with one straight edge really draws the eye to the straight line—the tape.

## Colors:
The color scheme is monochromatic—white, black, and a few grays where the light illuminates the black or shadows the white tape roll. There is a lot of contrast between the white tape and the black dispenser, but there are also more subtle contrasts in the edge of the dispenser (where the light makes the edges a lighter color). The overall effect is severe, but with a little softness from the translucency of the tape and from the soft lighting.

But if I were changing the color scheme, I'd rebel against the black and white and do it in Mondrian blues and yellows in a geometric pattern.

But if I were incorporating it into a woven piece, I'd try for something softly monochromatic with patches of white, pale gray, charcoal gray, and black. Maybe a plaid scarf in those colors, with a touch of red to brighten it up?

## Textures:
The tape dispenser has more interesting textures than I thought! The sides are lightly roughened, probably to make picking it up easier, but the top surface is quite smooth. The tape feels smooth initially, but has a slight "tooth" that makes it possible to write on it. It's definitely not the slick, mirror-finish tape you find sometimes. And, of course, there is a rough, toothy edge at the tape-cutting end.

I'm intrigued by the difference in texture between the smooth top of the tape dispenser and the rough dispensing edge. It presents a profound contrast that I find very appealing. Perhaps I could incorporate some rough metal bits into a woven piece, to provide texture? It wouldn't need to be sharp, just rough enough to be interesting.

## Lines:

There are interesting curves around the outer edges—straight and smooth along the bottom and the side edges, but intriguingly swoopy and curvy as you go along the top. There is also a straight line in the tape as it travels from roll to cutter, and circular lines in the tape roll, echoed in the tape-roll holder.

None of these lines especially inspires me, but I do find the juxtaposition between curved and straight lines interesting. It might be interesting to try a piece that combines straight lines and curves.

## Function:

The tape dispenser, not too surprisingly, is there to dispense tape, so the user can bind things together. But it could be used for other things: as a paperweight, as a weapon (it's quite heavy), or even as a very small flower pot, perhaps for tiny "air plant" bromeliads. If painted bright colors, it could make a very attractive (and unusual) pot.

## Free association on object:

Tape, gag (mouth taped shut), red tape, taping things together. Love is like tape—it fastens things together. Velcro. Black and white colors—old photos, TVs, newspapers.

## Most interesting ideas:

- Monochromatic black and white color scheme (maybe with a touch of color)
- Contrasting straight lines and curves
- Mondrian color scheme
- Contrast between rough metal and smooth rest of piece
- Velcro as a material
- Letting a piece "speak" as opposed to "gagging" it with functional requirements
- Design ideas:
  - Scarf in monochromatic shades of white, light gray, dark gray, and black, with a red accent
  - Something in bright geometric shapes in contrasting colors, with both straight lines and swoopy curves
  - Soft fabric mixed with rough metal bits—could be incorporated into a piece about mental illness?
  - Some kind of artistic gag, perhaps a gag that has something written or drawn on it, so it can "speak"?

Once you've learned to look closely at things around you, you'll find that generating new ideas is a snap. Capture them in an idea notebook—physical or electronic—and you'll be ready for the next step, designing your project.

# FUNCTIONAL DESIGN

Designing a useful piece is like writing a mystery novel. You'll need to answer four questions in order to create a good design:

1. Who is the piece for? (If you plan to sell it, who is your buyer? Who will use it?)
2. Why would someone want to purchase or use this piece? (And why do you want to make it?)
3. What am I making?
4. How will I make it?

In this chapter, we'll discuss *Who*, *Why*, and the functional aspects of *What*.

## WHO

In general, there are three people whose needs are relevant to the making of a piece: the purchaser, the user, and you. Your work needs to offer value to at least one of these in order to be worth making.

Start by understanding whose needs are paramount. If you are making the piece just to suit your own tastes—to explore a technique, or as an avenue for artistic self-expression— then you need not consider the priorities of the buyer, or even the user. (If that is the case, skip to chapter 5, "Visual Design.") But if you are not making a piece exclusively for yourself, knowing the tastes and budget of the person who will buy your product is critical to designing something that will sell. Even if you are gifting your work, you'll want to know who will use it and for what purpose, so you can create something that will be appreciated and used. That may mean subordinating your own tastes to those of the recipient. You may love purple, but if your friend hates it, she probably won't wear your exquisite amethyst necklace, no matter how much time and skill you put into making it.

While you do not *need* to be customer focused to produce and sell good work, you will likely earn more from your craft if you set out to make your work appeal to customers. Think about how you want to balance artistic freedom against sales. There is no right or wrong answer to this question. Selling craftwork in an age of cheap manufactured goods is difficult. Making a living by doing so is even harder. If you plan to sell substantial amounts of craftwork, you'll definitely want to be aware of what your customers will buy and how they will use what they buy.

To understand the market, ask yourself about your purchaser's tastes and lifestyle. What values does your shopper have around his or her purchases? Does your buyer want only the best, or something affordable? Is artistic expression more important, or practicality for daily use? Understanding your purchaser's values and personal style will help you design something that fits the buyer's needs.

One of the best ways to get information is simply to talk to your potential customers. If you are selling at or attending craft shows, chat with people. Even casual conversation can tell you a lot about their values and personal style. Also observe the people who buy. What are they wearing, and what do they look like? What does that tell you about their tastes and values?

# WHY

Once you understand whose needs are most important, think about why that person would benefit from your work. If you are making a piece for yourself, what are you hoping to get out of it? Perhaps you want to explore an idea, a material, or a technique. Or perhaps you simply need something useful—a set of placemats, or dinnerware, to fill a functional need.

If you are making a piece for someone else, ask yourself why that person would want to buy or use your work. What problems do they want your product to solve? What needs will it fill? How will it improve his or her life?

Don't think about your piece in a vacuum. Look at other pieces with a similar function. Ask yourself what makes your piece superior to something mass-manufactured, or something made by another artisan.

I had a long-standing argument with a woman who felt that anything handmade was inherently better than something manufactured, because of the hands-on quality of handmade items. And I always said to her, "No, no, no. I don't think that's true. Handmade is fine, but good design is good design. I'd rather have a well-designed coffee mug from a big box store than a poorly designed mug from some potter down the street that falls apart and feels lousy against your mouth."

*Rachel Carren, polymer artist*

Rachel Carren. *Bonnard Cupola Brooch*, 2010. Polymer, acrylic pigment, mica powder. 2.31" × 2.31" × 0.31". *Photographer: Hap Sakwa.*

# WHAT: FUNCTIONAL DESIGN

The third consideration of your design process is *What*. This is the blueprint, the design for your piece. In this section, we'll consider the functional aspects of design.

Once you understand why your piece will be valuable to the end user, mentally walk through how he or she will use it. Then think about how well your piece fulfills the intended use. For example, if you are making a custom rocking chair, imagine someone sitting in it. Is it comfortable both stationary and rocking? Is the seat length appropriate for the legs of the person sitting in it? Can it be cleaned easily? If the user is heavy, how sturdy does it need to be?

Thinking about how the object will be used will give you a better idea of how it needs to function.

Mea Rhee. *Bowls with Chopsticks*, 2015. Wheel-thrown stoneware with hand-cut rims. 6.5" × 4" × 6.5". *Photographer: Mea Rhee.*

My most popular design is a bowl that is designed to hold a pair of chopsticks on its rim. That's not an uncommon idea. You see a lot of potters making bowls that are intended to hold chopsticks, but mine are different because I try to design them so that if you use them with utensils other than chopsticks, they don't look weird. They still look normal, whereas other bowls that I see that are meant to hold chopsticks, they look like they are so specifically designed for chopsticks that other utensils look weird. I didn't want that. That was a large factor in the design of the bowl.

Another design factor was that I wanted it to be used while sitting on your couch in front of the TV. Therefore, it's meant to be held in one hand while you eat with the other. Over time, the shape of the bowl actually morphed a little bit. It became taller and narrower, and that was specifically for the function of eating on your sofa. A deeper bowl is less likely to spill stuff.

*Mea Rhee, potter*

By visualizing someone using your work, you can see what characteristics would be useful, and build them into your design.

Even better than visualization, of course, is watching someone use your work, or else using it yourself. This may not be practical if you are making one-of-a-kind pieces, but if you are developing a product line, asking others to test it is critical to creating a useful product. If your needs are similar to the customer's, you can also use the piece yourself to test out its practicality.

I buy a lot of pottery, and I use pottery every day, so I consider myself a pretty educated customer. A lot of my pottery designs start with, "What would I use? What do I need?" That's where I start from.

*Mea Rhee, potter*

---

Be careful when using yourself as an example customer, though. Basing your design around your own needs only works if your needs are similar to those of your customers. If you're designing a yoga mat, and you're not a yoga enthusiast, don't try to guess based on your own tastes. Instead, ask some yoga practitioners to test your mat before you sell it.

---

## EXERCISE 2: GETTING FEEDBACK FROM USERS

If your piece is intended to be functional, take one of your pieces to someone who is likely to use it (or a similar product)—perhaps a customer, perhaps a friend. Ask that person to try out your work. Ideally, watch him or her using it. Keep an eye out for stumbling blocks or problems: a shawl so slippery it doesn't stay on, a basket whose handle is too small to grip comfortably, a wine glass that knocks over easily. Watching someone use your product will give you a better sense for how it fares in practice.

Next, ask the person testing your product to take a piece home and use it for a while, then tell you what he or she thinks is good and what could be improved. This will let you know how your work functions when used in daily life. (Because this requires some effort on the part of your trial user, some return favor may be in order, especially if you are asking a stranger to evaluate your work.)

Finally, try using your piece yourself. This is the simplest method but not always the most accurate one, as you are already familiar with your work. Because you know your piece's design and intended purpose, you may automatically work around flaws in its functional design. And because you have designed it, it is likely to be sized and shaped to fit your needs. But using your own work will give you a much deeper understanding of its usability than observing someone else using it, or getting a report from someone who's tried it. It's also a lot easier to do, since you need not involve anyone else.

# DESIGN ASPECTS TO CONSIDER

When thinking about functional design, here are some common aspects to evaluate:

First, consider *utility*. An object should work as intended—a plate holds food, and a teapot pours tea. (Even a decorative piece has functional requirements: it needs to be easy to hang or display.) For a piece that will see daily use, it should also be easy to clean or care for. An heirloom christening wrap might be used and cleaned once per generation, so dry-clean-only is fine. A baby blanket for everyday use, however, will likely get lots of baby-related stains, and need to be cleaned daily—preferably in a washing machine.

Next, consider *ergonomics*. A product intended for use must be comfortable in the hand or against the body, and during its intended use. If it isn't, think about how you can redesign it to make it better balanced and easier to use.

Is it comfortable to hold? If it's a pot that needs to move, like a teapot or a pitcher, is it comfortable to move it? Does it feel balanced? Can you put it in a dishwasher? That's extremely important to me. Is it going to be durable enough to use on a daily basis? Will it outlive the person who owns it? That's really important to me, too.

*Mea Rhee, potter*

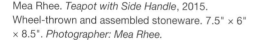

Mea Rhee. *Teapot with Side Handle*, 2015.
Wheel-thrown and assembled stoneware. 7.5" × 6" × 8.5". *Photographer: Mea Rhee.*

*Longevity* is important to consider, too. Some materials degenerate over time—silk becomes brittle, dyes fade, metal tarnishes. If you are planning an heirloom piece, you need to consider how your piece will hold up over the generations, and choose your materials and construction accordingly. If, on the other hand, you are making a trendy style of clothing that will only be worn for only one season, longevity is not an issue.

A piece also needs to have appropriate *durability*. Your piece should be able to stand up to the rigors of normal use. Does it need to be washed repeatedly? Will it be spilled on, rubbed against, exposed to sunlight? A piece that gets relatively little wear doesn't need to be as tough as a piece that is used in daily life. Heirloom china, for example, doesn't get used often and is generally handled carefully, so can be more delicate than restaurant dinnerware, which is used several times a day, washed in a commercial dishwasher, and is apt to be dropped on the floor.

Take a moment and consider how your piece is most likely to meet its end. Thinking about things that will destroy your piece may bring up ideas for better design. For example, if you expect a pitcher to break if dropped, you might consider making it more shatter-resistant, or less likely to be dropped. To accomplish this, you could put a stronger handle on it, or roughen the outer surface to make it easier to hold, or make it thicker and harder to break.

Consider any *special constraints* on the piece—the shape of an object to be used in a worship service, for example, or the fiber content and color of a Jewish tallit. If you are making a piece for a charity organization, they may have specific requests, depending on the charity's mission or the item's purpose. Take into account any special requirements when reviewing your design.

Also consider any legal requirements for the piece. Does it need to be tested for flammability or strength? Do you need to put a label on the piece, and if so, what needs to be on the label? Some research now can save you from a lot of grief later.

There are many considerations for functional design—too many to list here. But the essence of creating a useful piece is to put yourself in the recipient's shoes, walk through the use of the object in daily life, and make sure the design is up to the job. Do this, and you'll likely create a piece that is both appreciated and used.

Designing a chair is really hard. First of all, it must be attractive, otherwise people will not buy it. Second, it needs to be sturdy, and last a really long time. Third, it must be able to be manufactured simply and economically. Fourth, ergonomics and comfort is crucial. Fifth, consideration must be given to what materials are the most environmentally friendly. Sixth, recycling after its useful life must also be considered. All these criteria must come together to form a useful beauty. A chair is a really complex thing for one person to design. I love the challenge of it. I think it's fun.

*Peter Danko, furniture designer*

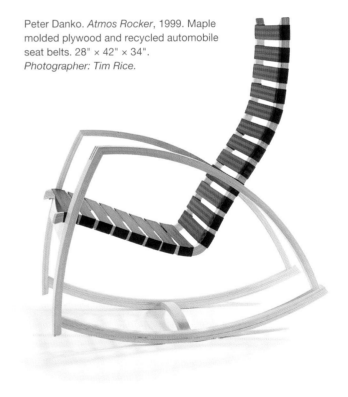

Peter Danko. *Atmos Rocker*, 1999. Maple molded plywood and recycled automobile seat belts. 28" × 42" × 34".
*Photographer: Tim Rice.*

# 5

# VISUAL DESIGN

Once you've thought through the functional design of a piece, think about the appearance. Visual design is a huge topic, which can't be fully covered in a single chapter. So instead of an extended discussion of two- and three-dimensional design, we'll look at two frameworks for thinking about visual design. The first is two factors you should consider when designing the appearance of your work, and the second is a helpful way to think about visual design.

## THE FACTORS

### Context

The first thing you need to know about your piece is whether it is the main character or the supporting cast in the story. It is easy to design a piece that shows off your prowess in your medium, but which doesn't satisfy its visual function. For example, a dramatic garment that doesn't flatter the wearer misses a critical element of visual design. If the primary intent is to show off your talent—on the haute couture runway, for example—this may not be a major flaw. But if your piece is not the diva, you'll want to think about harmonizing with the rest of the cast, and supporting the piece that is the central focus.

So if you are making tableware, consider how well it will coordinate with everything else on the table. A dramatic placemat may look good by itself, but may cause visual confusion if combined with clashing china. Similarly, jewelry needs to flatter the wearer, and coordinate with other items being worn.

Of course, you may not know the entire context of the piece before making it, particularly if you are making items for sale. But put some thought into its likely context, based on what you know (or have surmised) about your end user.

Mea Rhee. *Enormous Coffee Mugs*, 2015. Wheel-thrown stoneware with wet-pulled handles. 6" × 4" × 5", 20 oz. capacity. *Photographer: Mea Rhee.*

I make all of my pottery gray. First, because those are my favorite colors: grays and browns, neutral earthy tones. But I also believe that the color gray fits in with any other color, so it's easy for people to buy my work and fit it in with everything else they already have, no matter how colorful it is.

*Mea Rhee, potter*

## Message

Every piece conveys a message. It can be an explicit message, such as an image or a symbol, or it can simply be the feeling a viewer gets when regarding your piece. Is your piece about classic, understated elegance? Then choose conservative color combinations, and a clean, simple style. Conversely, if you are trying to set a jazzy mood, use bright colors with plenty of contrast to raise the energy of a piece.

If possible, your message should harmonize with the mood of the piece's surroundings. In general, an ensemble—whether a set of garments and jewelry or an entire room—should be "about" one thing, and each element of the ensemble should support the theme.

# THE VISUAL STORY

Once you've decided on context and message, it's time to think about the visual "story" you are telling—the way the viewer's eye moves through your piece.

How does this work? Well, a viewer's eye doesn't take in an entire piece at once. Instead, the eye looks first at the most attention-grabbing spot. Then it travels through the piece, taking in the other points of interest as it goes. By giving the eye subtle cues about where to go and what to focus on, you can guide the viewer through the piece. In short, you are telling the viewer a story—visually.

So think about the components of a good story. Start with a collection of characters—a few lead characters and a supporting cast—written in a consistent and engaging style. Then you'll want a compelling plot, with a strong beginning and a clear ending. And you'll want it to meld seamlessly into a unified whole.

A well-designed craft piece tells that story visually. The characters are its attention-grabbing areas, and the plot is the way the viewer's eye travels between them. The journey of the eye, from the instant it enters the piece to the moment that it leaves, becomes your story.

Let's construct the story.

## Elements as characters

The first thing you need to tell your visual story is a cast of characters, otherwise known as *elements*. These are the parts of your piece that you want people to look at, the things that stand out as worthy of the eye's attention. They are the points of interest that the eye will visit during its journey through your piece.

For example, in figure 5-1, the elements are the pink dots. They stand out among the sea of gray dots, and your eye looks there first.

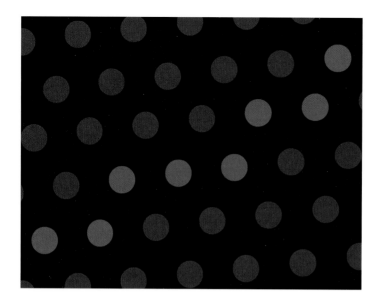

FIGURE 5-1. The pink dots are the elements.

But wait! There is something lacking in its story. All the elements are the same, and attract the eye equally. As a result, the piece feels incomplete and unfocused.

What if we make one of the elements stronger than the others?

FIGURE 5-2. The yellow dot is the focal point.

Now the story feels more satisfying—it has a visual climax, a central focus.

## Focal point = main character

Unless you are specifically creating a work without a focus, such as a traditional quilt with identical blocks, your piece will work better if there is a single, primary element that acts as a main character. This is usually called the *focal point*. The other elements play a supporting role, drawing the eye through the rest of the piece. However, too many elements can create visual confusion, especially if they are all equally strong. Typically, you don't want a crowd of characters with equal emphasis; you want a main character and a supporting cast.

### Using contrast to establish focal point

What makes you look at the yellow dot—or the pink ones, for that matter? What makes them so enticing to the eye?

It's because they *contrast* with the gray dots in the background. The brain seeks out visual patterns, and will spot exceptions to a pattern instantly. If you establish a pattern and then break it with something different, the eye will fixate on the part that is different. The higher the contrast, the more strongly it draws the eye. In the example above, the pink dots contrast with the gray dots, and the yellow dot contrasts with both the pink and the gray. The yellow dot is different from all the others, so it draws the eye.

Contrast doesn't have to be color. It can be shape, size, position, style—or many other things. To create contrast, establish a pattern and break it. The eye will go to whatever breaks the pattern. Figures 5-3 through 5-6 show some ways to establish elements and focal points through contrast.

FIGURE 5-3. Using shape to establish focal point/elements.

FIGURE 5-4. Using size to establish focal point/elements.

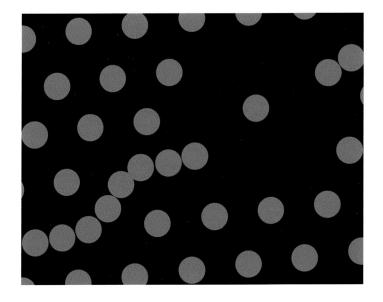

FIGURE 5-5. Using position to establish focal point/elements.

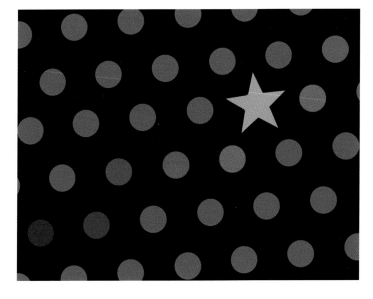

FIGURE 5-6. Using color to establish elements and shape to create a focal point.

## Using placement of focal point

Contrast isn't the only way to establish your main character. Placement can help establish a focal point, too.

The strongest placement of a focal point is dead center. Putting something interesting in the center of a piece will draw the eye inexorably to that something. Is that good? It depends on what else you want the eye to see. Unless managed carefully, a focal point at the center will completely dominate a piece. If you are creating something where you want the eye in the center—something like a mandala, for example—centering your focal point is a good idea. It can also work for symmetric pieces, especially radially symmetric pieces. Otherwise, it's best to put the focal point off center, so the eye can travel through the rest of the piece.

Consider figure 5-7, which has its focal point at the center.

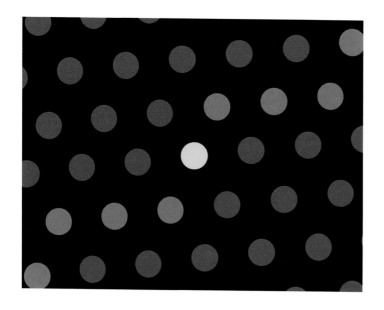

FIGURE 5-7. Focal point placed in center.

In this drawing, the eye gets "stuck" on the focal point and doesn't leave it readily, resulting in a stiff, formal feel. Contrast this with the off-center focal point in figure 5-8—the off-center focus point is much more dynamic and intriguing than the centered one.

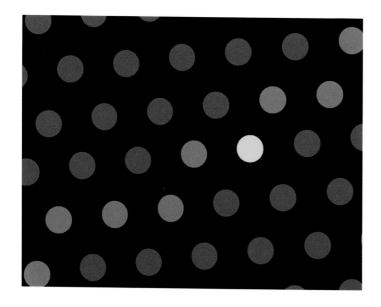

FIGURE 5-8. Focal point placed off center.

This does not mean that you should never place a focal point at the center. Whether you choose to place it on or off center depends entirely on what kind of mood or impression you are trying to achieve, and on the visual balance of the piece. For example, many beautiful quilts have fourfold or radially symmetric patterns with a center focal point, which enhances rather than detracts from the design. But a center focal point combined with symmetry produces a very formal feeling, while an off-center focal point produces a more informal, dynamic feel.

## Using the rule of thirds

The rule of thirds provides another helpful guideline for focal point placement. If you place a grid over a piece that divides it into thirds, vertically and horizontally, placing a focal point at the intersection of the gridlines will make it more visually satisfying. Figures 5-9 and 5-10 show a focal point that follows the rule of thirds—it's located near one of the intersections on the grid. Figures 5-11 and 5-12 show a focal point that does not follow the rule of thirds. The focal point looks more natural in Figure 5-9.

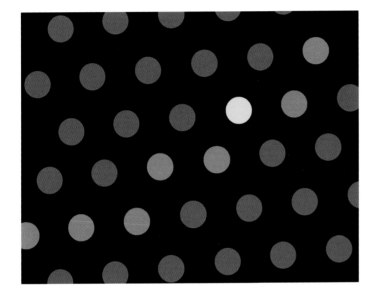

FIGURE 5-9. Focal point placed according to Rule of Thirds.

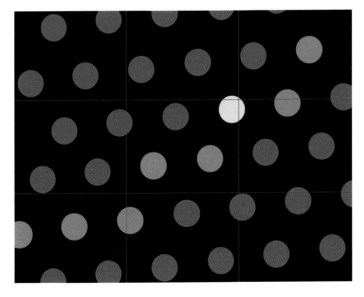

FIGURE 5-10. Grid lines for a focal point that follows the Rule of Thirds.

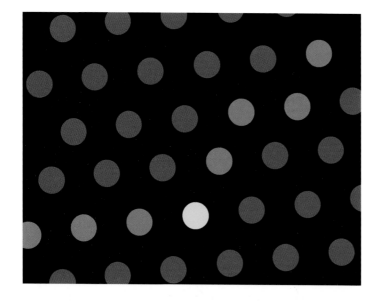

FIGURE 5-11. Focal point that does not follow the Rule of Thirds.

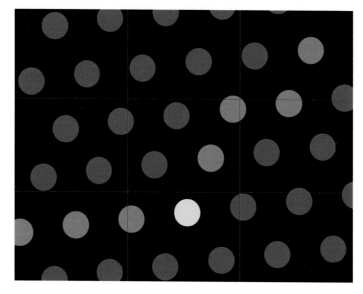

FIGURE 5-12. Grid lines for a focal point that does not follow the Rule of Thirds.

## Unity of style

In addition to the cast of characters, *style* is also part of your visual story. For a more unified piece, elements should be stylistically related. You wouldn't want to read a book where the first chapter was a gripping thriller, the second chapter an oozy romance, and the third chapter an academic text. Similarly, your piece will hold together better if you give its elements unity of style. If your focal point is a shape of some sort, think about making your other elements shapes as well. If your focal point is about line, make the other elements about line. Shifting styles abruptly will jar the viewer. Consider the example in figure 5-13—there is no unity, no consistency of style between elements, resulting in a chaotic and disjointed effect. If that is what you want, great. But if not, use a more consistent style.

FIGURE 5-13. Inconsistent styles produce visual chaos.

## Opening scene = entry point

Once you've established your cast of characters, it's time to think about the plot of your visual story. Where do you want the eye to enter? Where do you want it to exit? What do you want it to see in between?

The entry point is the first thing you see when you look at the piece. It's the most attention-grabbing part of the piece, often the focal point, and it typically jumps out at you from a distance. From the entry point, the eye tours the rest of the piece, taking in the other elements, until it exits the piece. By connecting your focal point and your elements, you can guide the eye from one spot to another, telling your visual story.

Where the eye enters a piece is influenced by culture. In Western culture, by default, the eye starts at the top left of an image. Because most Western cultures read from left to right and top to bottom, the Western eye automatically starts where it would naturally begin reading—the top left. (This is why websites written in English universally place their logos in the top left.) This doesn't mean that the entry point is always there. But if you plan to have your entry point at the bottom right, it will have to be much stronger to overcome that natural draw.

## Plot = transition
## between elements

After the entry point, where does the eye look next? Ah, there's the *plot* of your visual story. If you gently guide the eye among the elements, your plot—and your piece—will flow more smoothly. And the viewer will see exactly what you are trying to show.

Elements can be connected in many ways. You can, of course, connect them literally, by drawing lines between them. In figure 5-14, subtle gray lines link the three colored squares.

FIGURE 5-14. Three elements connected by subtle gray lines.

FIGURE 5-15. Three elements connected by implied line.

You can also use implied line to connect your elements. In figure 5-15, no solid lines connect the elements, but the parallel brush strokes in the entry point (the large red square) point at the blue square, creating an implied line that guides the eye. The blue square points at the green square, keeping the eye moving from element to element.

You can create implied line in many different ways. For example, an arrow shape propels the eye in the direction of the arrow. Likewise, if you depict a person or an animal that is looking at an object, the line of sight creates an implied line that draws the viewer's eye to that object.

Another way to move the eye through the piece is to establish a natural progression. In figure 5-16, notice how the dots get progressively smaller as they snake around to the focal point, the smallest dot. The gradual reduction in dot size provides a natural progression that leads the eye from the bottom left to the focal point and creates a sense of movement in the piece.

FIGURE 5-16. Creating motion through a natural progression in size.

There are many other ways to create the plot of a visual story—far too many to cover here. But if you get in the habit of looking for the elements and focal point of a piece, and ask yourself how your eye moves through the piece, you'll get some wonderful ideas for guiding your viewers through your own visual story.

## Ending = exit point

The final plot consideration is how to end your story. The exit point is where the eye departs the piece. Unlike a written story, it doesn't have to be explicit, nor does it have to be on the edge—it's just a natural ending-point for the eye. In figure 5-17, for example, the exit point is the small leaf at the bottom right.

FIGURE 5-17. Drawing of leaves, with exit point at bottom right.

FIGURE 5-18. Drawing of leaves, exit point removed.

The eye enters at the top yellow leaf, and follows the drifting leaves down to the exit point at bottom right.

Figure 5-18 shows what happens if we remove the exit point.

Suddenly the piece feels less interesting, more static. The eye feels "trapped" within the piece.

In general, a piece that has elements only partially contained within the frame will be more visually interesting than a piece that is wholly within the frame. That's because an element crossing the border is intriguing—it's partially hidden—and also because it implies motion out of the frame. Of course, that does not mean you should place an element "on the edge" simply for the sake of doing so. But if you typically keep everything within a nice neat border, try letting an element flow out of the frame to see what happens.

# EXAMPLE: *AUTUMN SPLENDOR*

Let's see how this all comes together in a craft context. Here's my handwoven, hand-dyed coat, *Autumn Splendor*:

The focal point (and entry point) of this garment is the cluster of leaves at the top. The leaf cluster contrasts strongly with the yellow background, is bigger than the lower leaves, and is placed near the neckline, making it the primary focus. (The human eye is strongly drawn to faces, so anything placed near the neckline will naturally attract the eye.) After the eye takes in the cluster of leaves, an implied line—the tip of the middle leaf—points down towards the next leaf, which in turn guides the eye to the bottom leaf. From there, the eye swoops down the line between bright and dark sides, and exits where the line ends, at the bottom of the coat. This piece tells a strong visual story.

FIGURE 5-19. Tien Chiu. *Autumn Splendor,* 2012. Handwoven swing coat in wool and silk, size 12. *Photographer: Joe Decker.*

I hope these guidelines have given you some ideas for how to design the appearance of your piece. Please keep in mind that these guidelines are simply that—guidelines. For almost any design rule, an excellent design can be found that breaks that rule. But your piece will be stronger if you choose consciously when to depart from the guidelines. Know why you are choosing to do things differently, and what impact it will have on your finished piece.

Experimenting with your creations will help you develop your eye. Try multiple versions of your design, changing one thing each time. See which way works better. Look at other people's work. Does it work? Why does it work? Or if it doesn't work, how would you go about fixing it? Practicing design constantly will sharpen your eye and strengthen your work.

# EXERCISE 3: TRAINING THE EYE

Find an object that you like—either human-made or something from the natural world. If it is three-dimensional, look at it from all sides. Consider its visual story. Refer back to chapter 5, "Visual Design," and try to answer these questions:

1. Where does your eye naturally enter the piece?

2. Does it have a focal point? If so, what is it?

3. How does your eye move through the piece? What is the plot of the visual story?

4. How does the story end? Is there a clear end point? Does it need one?

5. What is the mood of the story? Is it cheerful and energetic, calm and meditative, or full of conflict? What aspects of the piece work together to convey that feeling?

6. Take a camera and snap a black-and-white photo of the piece. What (if anything) changed about the feel of the piece? Do you see interesting shapes and lines now that the distraction of color has been eliminated?

7. Look at the object again, after examining the black-and-white photo. How does color change the piece? How has color been used to set the mood or guide your eye between elements?

8. What do you think is effective about the visual design of the piece? What elements speak to you most strongly?

9. What do you think is ineffective? What elements do you find distracting?

Examining designs in the world around you—both human-made and natural—will build your design vocabulary, and sharpen your eye for what works (and doesn't work) in your own pieces.

# 6

# GETTING STARTED

Once you have some idea of the *Who, Why,* and *What* of a project, dive into designing your next piece. You can do this in one of two ways: improvise, or develop a design in advance.

## IMPROVISING

One approach, particularly if you have a good idea of what you want already, is simply to dive in. Stick the idea in the back of your head, take out some materials or a sketch pad, and work spontaneously until you arrive at an end result you like. You can explore the medium, experimenting with new materials or brewing up a new combination of familiar ingredients. Or you can pick a technique and see where it takes you.

Once I conceive an idea and direction that I want to go, I tend to chew on it for a long time. I get pictorial visions in my head and I try to let them expand as time goes on. When I am fairly sure they have the possibility to work in the medium, I warp up the loom, sit down and start weaving.

I keep a sketchbook and I sketch all the time, but I don't make a cartoon (an image to follow when weaving the tapestry). I find that my process is probably more related to telling a story or writing a narrative. I just start with an idea.

I have a vision that I'm aiming for, but then once I start weaving, I let it grow within the process. Tapestry weaving is very slow and you spend a lot of time on detail, so there is lots of time to let the story develop and the narrative expand. It is an exciting way to work.

*Susan Martin Maffei, tapestry weaver*

Susan Martin Maffei working on the piece *New York Times Series—Travel.* Photographer: Archie Brennan.

# BRAINSTORMING DESIGNS

If you prefer to plan in advance, start filling in *What* by brainstorming some designs. In fact, brainstorm lots of designs, especially if you are embarking on a large project. The first—or even second or third—design is probably not going to be the strongest one, so generate tons of designs—good and bad—and then choose the best among them.

Don't be afraid to make many sketches. Put them aside if they don't work. Let one grow out of the one before until you can find something that you think is worth developing into the medium of tapestry. Ask the question "why weave it?" And don't be afraid to stop and then start the weaving again if it is not working.

*Susan Martin Maffei, tapestry weaver*

---

In *Think Better: An Innovator's Guide to Productive Thinking,*[1] Tim Hurson explains that the first third of a brainstorming session produces boring, predictable results. The second third begins to stretch the boundaries of the pedestrian. But the really innovative, interesting designs don't appear until the "third third," the end of a good brainstorming session. He says it's like water from a tap that hasn't been used for a while: before you can get to the cool, clear water, you have to run the tap to get rid of the gunk that's settled in the pipes. Similarly, to get to the most innovative, creative designs, you have to flush away the pedestrian ones first.

A good brainstorming session follows these four rules:[2]

1. No criticism. Don't judge your ideas while brainstorming. Shut off the analytic mind.

2. Welcome wild ideas. Wild ideas help you get off the beaten track and produce the most creative results.

3. Quantity over quality. The more ideas you generate, the better the chance of getting good designs.

4. Build on and combine ideas. Don't feel obligated to come up with 100% new designs; build on previously brainstormed designs, or combine elements from two or more designs.

The first rule is often the toughest to follow. We're accustomed to using the analytic mind, but in the context of brainstorming, it often acts as an internal censor. But saying "No, that won't work," or "That's a terrible idea!" will instantly shut down creative thought.

The left brain can be really critical. The left brain wants us to make sure that we're not making a fool of ourselves, that we're not making a mistake, or that we're doing the right thing. And it wants us to be safe.

Whereas the right side of the brain, the artistic side, is intuitive. It's the gut feeling, the visualization, the non-verbal communication, non-specific ideas.

The thing about the right brain is that it doesn't work under stress, it doesn't work when you're unhappy, and it doesn't work with negativity. And so the left brain can easily control and overwhelm the right brain. So many people, when they're trying to do something creative, are saying to themselves, "I can't do this right," or "I'm not creative," or "I'm not artistic." They're talking negatively about themselves to themselves.

Well, whatever you tell your brain, it's going to prove you right.

*Joen Wolfrom, quilter*

One way to shut down the internal censor is to impose a time limit, or target a certain number of designs. When brainstorming designs, I often use a game I call Design Poker, an adaptation of Anne Sutton and Diane Sheehan's "The Design Game."[3]

# EXERCISE 4: DESIGN POKER

Collect fifteen to twenty ideas and place each on a three-by-five-inch index card. An idea might be an inspirational image, a material to use in the piece, a concept or theme, a color scheme, a design element, or anything else that relates to the piece. You don't have to limit yourself to writing ideas—feel free to paste down images, make sketches, attach small objects, and so on.

Shuffle your cards and draw five cards at random. Set a timer for ten or fifteen minutes, and try to generate five or more unique designs before the timer rings. You will probably find that the first few design ideas come easily, but that after that, you briefly draw a blank. After that, the ideas will become progressively wilder and wilder as you flail about trying to generate a design—any design. That's great! You are flushing away the boring, predictable designs and getting to the interesting ones.

Repeat the game with a different set of cards until you feel you have brainstormed enough designs. Then choose five of your favorite designs and play Design Poker again, this time using the five designs as a starting point. This allows you to continue brainstorming, but this time building on and combining ideas.

Nothing about Design Poker is sacred, so create your own variants. You can play the same set of cards over and over, or choose five of your favorite ideas to work with rather than drawing cards at random. You can also work without a timer, though I urge you to try it with a timer first. The timer does two things: It helps turn off the inner critic, since you'll be in too much of a hurry to evaluate designs. And it helps keep you moving—otherwise the temptation is to stop and flesh out a single design instead of achieving your objective, which is to generate lots of ideas. If you do decide to work without a timer, increase the number of designs you create to help you exhaust all the "safe" ideas and get to the more creative ones.

Most of your brainstormed designs will be bad ones—and that's okay. In fact, it's desirable. You won't arrive at the most creative, original designs by playing it safe. Instead, reach for as many off-the-wall ideas as you can. You don't need every design to be good; you only need one good design. The way to get to that design is to create lots of designs—good and bad—and then select the good ones. You can always modify a design to make it more practical; it's very hard to make a conservative design more imaginative.

---

## FLESHING OUT YOUR DESIGN

Once you've brainstormed ideas, choose one that you like and start filling in some details. Feel free to use elements from other designs you brainstormed as you modify your selected design. You are not locked into the design you chose. Instead, use it as a starting point and modify it however you please.

As you are fleshing out the details, think about the *Who*, *Why*, and *What* for the piece. Gradually modify the design until it meets the requirements in *Why*, and is practical to construct.

## HOW FAR AHEAD SHOULD YOU PLAN?

There are advantages to keeping designs simple, and advantages to thinking everything through in advance. The more you plan, the better you can think ahead and anticipate problems. Planning reduces the odds of making a mistake—the higher the cost of a mistake, and the more likely you are to make one, the better off you are thinking through your design.

But planning out everything beforehand can also destroy spontaneity, producing a piece that feels stiff and stilted. It's also easy to get into "analysis paralysis," where you get so caught up in critiquing and changing your designs that you never get around to making anything. And if you discover something new, or decide to change the design on the fly, the time put into your previous design will be wasted.

So the best strategy for design is to plan just as far ahead as you are likely to adhere to that design while making the project. That could be the entire layout of the piece, or it could be just choosing some materials with which to improvise. Doing "just enough" design allows you to think through some problems in advance while retaining flexibility and avoiding wasted time.

How much design you want to start with also depends on the medium. Some media require decisions to be made up front. For example, when weaving, you need to measure your warp threads and put them onto the loom before you can begin weaving cloth. As a result, weavers need to make significant decisions before setting up a new project, deciding the type and quantity of cloth they plan to produce, and narrowing their choices for the structural design of the fabric. Other media are more suited to improvisation, and projects can start with just a few quick choices.

What you're making also matters. In general, complex projects and projects that have little room for error are better suited for thought-through designs. Building an ornate cabinet requires more precise assembly than carving a simple wooden spoon, so it benefits from early design sketches. And a ring made of platinum will benefit from advance planning to avoid wasting expensive metal.

The materials have a lot to do with it. If you're saying, "Well, I've got a box full of a thousand bottle tops and I'm going to try to make jewelry out of it," well, what the heck, you know, let's just get started. Put on the music and go crazy and see what comes out. But if you've got a quarter-ounce of gold and you say, "I'm going to make a piece of jewelry out of this," obviously your approach is going to be a lot more careful, and you'd be more likely to do drawings or models or write out a script. Whatever form it takes, there's going to be more planning in a case like that.

*Tim McCreight, metalworker*

Consider your *Why* for the project. Are you seeking to understand a technique? Then you may not need an elaborate design—jumping in and playing spontaneously with the technique may help you discover things about it better than planning out an entire project. Similarly, if your primary intent is to express yourself spontaneously, diving in is great—it prevents you from overthinking. On the other hand, if your goal is a commissioned piece, you will usually want to start with some sketches to show the client.

Finally, consider your personal style. Some people like to plan everything, and others prefer to work in the moment, "going with the flow" rather than seeking to control the end result. Most people fall somewhere in between, of course, using either approach depending on their mood and their goals.

Your preference may also evolve over time. Most of the master artisans interviewed for this book described an evolution of their creative style. They went from planning projects and struggling to make their projects match their vision to more improvisational styles, "collaborating with" the medium rather than controlling it. As you gain experience, you may find yourself doing the same.

Tim McCreight. *Untitled (Knife)*, 2006. Steel, sterling silver, wood (maple), linen cord. Length: 5.5". *Photographer: Robert Diamante*.

I used to start by drawing. But now I don't. I found that I was in a more dynamic partnership with the tools and the materials when I didn't have a preconceived idea. I found myself wanting to step back a bit and say, "Okay, what does the metal want to do? What does this tool bring to the party today? What marks are being made, what forms are being created?"

It's a little bit like a collaboration. If you were a textiles person and a store contacted you and said, "I've got a window on Main Street, and we want you and two other people—a graphic designer, and a metalworker—to decorate it," you could say, "Okay, I can do that."

And then if you go into that collaboration and you say, "Okay, guys, I've got it—here's exactly what we're going to do," they're going to say "Well, what do you need me for?"

They aren't going to be very happy. And you've immediately shut off the possibility of whatever they were going to bring—their particular talents and visions, right? So you wouldn't do that.

If I said, "We're going to collaborate, and I'm in charge," right away you'd say, "Whoa! That doesn't sound like collaboration."

So, the way I work now, I like to think of it as a collaboration with the material and the tools, and drawing does not typically help that.

Now, I do have one caveat to that. I think it's really important to have an element of control first. I don't think you can have the confidence needed until you have proven to yourself you are in control. So I would say to a student, a beginning metalworker, "Okay, we're going to see if you can map out these steps. You're going to come up with an idea and you're going to show me what that idea is. Then we're going to talk through the steps, you're going to make that piece, and then we're going to compare where you ended up with where you started."

And the goal in one's early education is that they will match. Perfectly. Now this might not be the most creative thing to do. Let's say the person says, "I'm going to make a disc that's exactly two inches in diameter, and it's going to have a one-inch perfect square sawn out of the middle."

Okay, that's good. It's boring. It's not going to be a piece of work that ends up in a museum. But it's going to be a great exercise because the student is going to walk through the steps, and at the end of the day we're going to be able to compare the drawing to the finished piece.

Then the student can say, "Wow! I really know how to manage my tools. I am in charge here. I have confidence that I can cut a straight line and I can file a smooth curve." And that's really important. I think you have to get to that point. And then you can let it go.

*Tim McCreight, metalworker*

# WHAT IF YOU'RE STUCK FOR IDEAS?

Practically every artist gets stuck for ideas at some point. The dry spell can be a few hours, a few days, or even months. It's perfectly normal to get stuck every once in a while.

The important part—advised by every artist interviewed for this book—is to work through it. Don't abandon your studio just because you don't have an idea, or don't feel inspired. Go make something—anything. Keep your hands moving. In time, ideas will come to you.

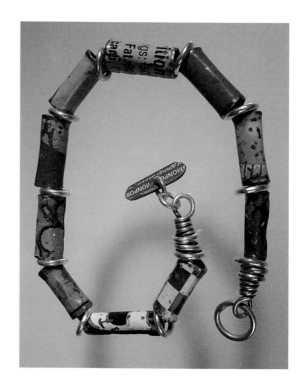

Ellen Wieske. *Tin Tube Bracelet*, 2001.
Tin and sterling silver. 0.25" × 6".
Photographer: Ellen Wieske.

When my father died about ten years ago, I was devastated. I didn't have any ideas. I didn't have anything I wanted to make. I didn't know what to do. But I had [a commitment to studio time] so I would go to my studio every day. For a couple of weeks, I didn't do anything. I cleaned my studio, I organized things, and eventually I just sat. And I thought, "I have to do something."

So I started to cut up some metal and I cut little rectangles. I cut hundreds of little rectangles with absolutely no clue as to what I would do with them, or why I was doing it, but I needed to fill my eight hours in the studio.

And then I started to roll them into tubes. These were little pieces of tin and so I started to make these little tubes and pretty soon I had this giant mayonnaise jar full of these little tin tubes. Weeks and weeks later, as I started to come out of the grief process, I had all these materials and it turned into a whole body of work. I don't think I ever would have gotten to another place if I hadn't stuck to my conviction that there is no excuse not to work.

Whether I have an idea or not, that's what I do. I go to my studio and I do something. And a lot of work has come out of just going to the studio, not having any idea what I'm going to do, and then noticing something, playing around with something, rearranging something. From that, an idea always comes.

*Ellen Wieske, metalworker*

The first thing I would say to a beginner is, "Work through it. Work through it—don't take the easy way out. Find some way to work even if that work is simple stuff. Maybe just cleaning your studio, but still you're there, you're in the studio. You're working."

Now eventually, you get to a point where you think, "This is just stupid. I'm just wasting my time. And if I keep doing this I'm just going to mess up fifty dollars' worth of silver and I'll have to start over again tomorrow." You'd be crazy if you didn't develop a radar for those moments also. I think you get it, but you get it with experience.

*Tim McCreight, metalworker*

Once you've found your idea and brainstormed your design, you'll want to think about how you plan to make it.

# PRACTICAL CONSIDERATIONS

Now that you've settled *Who*, *Why*, and *What*, the next step is to figure out *How* you will make your new design. Start by finding out whether you can make it at all. On paper, you can design anything. But working with actual materials is different—some things are impossible, others are only possible with elaborate contortions, expensive equipment, or lots of skill. So after you rough out the visual and functional design, think about the practical aspects—how you're going to make it. Here are a few areas to consider.

## CONSTRUCTABILITY

First, consider the engineering of the piece. Can it be made at all? Walk yourself through the creation of the piece, one step at a time, noting down any questions you have along the way. What skills and tools do you need to make it? What materials do you plan to use?

We have an idea in our minds—or maybe there's a drawing on a piece of paper. But in actuality, depending on the fabric, whether it's sheer or heavy, what fiber it's made from, the type of dye application, you get different results.

I tell students to try different substrates—paper, cloth that's sheer. There are ways of working with polyester. Polyester is interesting. What are the qualities of the material?

*Ana Lisa Hedstrom, surface design artist*

If you're not sure whether something is constructible, and you don't want to experiment to find out for yourself, find someone who does have the expertise to know. This is not nearly as daunting as it sounds: social networks, online communities, mailing lists, YouTube videos, and search engines make finding answers far easier today than thirty years ago. Books and classes help, too.

Perhaps you'll realize that your design is not constructible as it stands. Good! It's better to find that out now than halfway through making it, when you've already invested lots of time. Now you can modify your design to make construction more feasible. Move into the Change step of the Creative Cycle (outlined in Chapter 2) and modify your design to make construction more feasible.

If it turns out that your design can be constructed, it's time to think about two questions. Do you have the wherewithal—skills, tools, materials, time, and stamina—to do the job? And will the project be worth the price of making it, both in time and money?

# SKILLS

After roughing out the design of a piece, think about the skills you'll need. At the outset of a project, you might just think about the broad strokes—if you're sewing a complicated jacket, for example, you'll need general sewing and fitting skills, and probably some knowledge of tailoring. As you develop the piece, you'll find yourself knowing more and more about the skills needed to construct it.

You do not need all the required skills before starting the project. In fact, if you already have all the required skills, you are probably not stretching yourself enough. However, you do need to be able to acquire those skills during the project—either by developing them yourself, or by finding someone to help you out. If you can't do either, you'll need to change that part of your design so it falls within your skills, or else accept that you may make mistakes in that portion of the piece. An error in one section need not be a disaster, however. Chapter 8, "Constructing Your Piece," contains some design strategies for reducing the negative impact of risky parts.

How far outside your skill level can you stretch your design? It depends on how fast you learn and how much risk you're willing to take. The further you stretch your skills, the more likely you are to make a mistake. Of course, if you never stretch yourself, you'll never grow your abilities, and the more skills you develop, the better your pieces can become. So it's a trade-off. If you are working with very expensive materials, or working within a short timeframe, be more conservative about stretching yourself because mistakes could spell disaster. On the other hand, if you are working with inexpensive materials and have plenty of time, you can really push your limits.

That said, don't try to learn everything at once. If you find yourself stretching your limits in too many areas, your project is unlikely to be successful.

When you're going to do a project, there should only be one major learning area in that project. If you're trying to work on color, design, and technique at the same time, that will overwhelm you. So if you want to learn about a new technique, let that be the focus. Everything else should be something that you're comfortable with. If you want to do something new with design, then the technical aspects should be something you're comfortable with.

*Joen Wolfrom, quilter*

# TOOLS

You will need tools to build your project. And some tools can be pretty pricey. To determine your tool costs, walk through the construction of your piece, identifying the tools you need for the job. If you can't afford (or don't want to buy) a given tool, think of ways to work around the missing tool, either by substituting another tool or by modifying your design.

# MATERIALS

Once you've covered skills and tools, consider your materials. Make a mental list of the materials needed in the piece. Then ask yourself a few questions:

*Are your materials up to their job?* For each ingredient, consider what it contributes to the piece and whether it has the characteristics it needs. For example, a patio chair must endure weather and sun. So it needs to be strong, durable against the elements, and not easily damaged by light exposure. It must also be pleasing to the eye. Figure out what characteristics you need, then check whether the materials can do it.

*Can you afford the materials needed?* There's no point in starting a project that you can't afford to finish, unless you think you can raise money halfway through. However, you may be able to create your design by substituting less expensive materials, or by finding a cheaper source.

*Are there more appropriate materials for the job?* You don't always need the highest-quality supplies for the job. Instead, choose the most appropriate materials. Unless you are really wealthy, you won't want to use expensive lace on a summer dress for a four-year-old; it will probably get stained, and the child will grow out of it so rapidly that the money will be wasted. Imported French lace might indeed look better, but an inexpensive, machine-made lace would be more appropriate. There may also be more durable or better-looking materials around. It's worth checking to see if better choices are available.

Your materials analysis doesn't have to take a long time. As you gain experience, and learn more about materials for your craft, you can go down your list of materials quickly, mentally ticking off each element.

# TIME

Another construction consideration is time. How long will it take to make the piece? Will you be able to get that present done by the holidays, or that exhibition piece done by the show entry deadline? Taking a moment to consider timing can save you from lots of late nights or missed deadlines.

Here are some suggestions that may help avoid unnecessary drama.

Start by estimating the effort. Take your best guess about how long each part of the construction process will take. Consider both the amount of effort—the number of working hours—it will take to complete each step, and the amount of time you can devote to that kind of work. (Even if you are a full-time artist, you may not have the mental energy to work on complicated designs for eight hours a day.) Don't get over-ambitious about devoting time to the project. If you typically spend three hours a day doing creative work, planning to work six hours a day probably won't work unless you make some major changes to your routine.

If you have no idea how long a step will take, you have two options. The first is to take your best guess. The second is to experiment with a small sample, measure how long it takes you to do that sample, and calculate the duration of the completed project from the time it took to do the sample. For example, if you are planning to stitch a quilt in a complex pattern, and you've never done it before, you could stitch a small area, timing yourself. Then estimate how much more you'll need to stitch, multiply by the amount of time it took you to do the sample, and you'll have a good starting estimate for the stitching time needed for the whole piece.

Mea Rhee in her studio. *Photographer: Mea Rhee.*

I have a pretty regimented production schedule. In every two-day cycle of work—one day throwing, one day trimming, and maybe some hand building—I know I can produce $1,250 worth of work. I have a whole bunch of to-do lists that add up to $1,250 worth of work. So in every two days of work, I finish one of those to-do lists. So when it comes to wholesale, I can look at the size of the wholesale order. A $500 order is actually $1,000 worth of pots because the wholesale price is roughly half retail. Then I know I can finish that in two days.

*Mea Rhee, potter*

Once you've made your estimate, add 30% to the amount of time you expect it to take. (Add 100% if you often underestimate your work time.) That's a ballpark figure; as you get more experience in estimation, you can change that number to something that more accurately reflects how you work. Adding extra time gives you a margin of safety, both for inaccurate estimates (people are notorious for underestimating the amount of effort involved in constructing anything) and for unexpected events such as illness or urgent other projects that may interrupt your work.

In addition to figuring out how many hours the project will take, consider how much time you have to work on the project. This depends partly on how much time you have available—jobs, kids, and other commitments often get in the way of creative time. It also depends on your stamina for project work. For example, if you are embarking on a sweater that will take forty hours to knit, you could conceivably knit it in a single week, but unless you are a really experienced knitter, your wrists and patience would likely give out partway through.

What if your project is extremely complex, and advance estimation is simply not possible? In those cases, break the project up into sub-projects, and take your best guess at estimating each sub-project. Then embark on the project, checking your estimates as you go. If the first few sub-projects are taking a really long time, longer than expected, you'll know you're in trouble and can simplify your design.

This may sound rather daunting, but with experience, the estimation process becomes faster. For simple projects, you can do it intuitively: "Yes, I've made three chairs, and they each took about three weeks. This chair is similar to the others, so it will probably also take three weeks, unless it's more complicated than I expect." For more complex projects, though, it's best to work through the estimates.

Finally, consider your stamina. Everyone has a different cadence to his or her craftwork. Some people are natural hares—they start projects quickly, but lose interest after a few days or weeks. Others, the tortoises, prefer longer projects, and don't mind spending months or years on a single project. The further you stretch your attention span, the more likely you are to wind up with unfinished projects.

That doesn't mean that you have to limit yourself to your usual project length, though. It just means you need to get creative about keeping your enthusiasm going. The easiest way to do that is to break a large project into smaller chunks, keeping each chunk small enough to accomplish. Then you don't need to finish the entire piece, just the next chunk. Essentially, you're breaking the project up into lots of small projects, small enough to fit your natural rhythm.

For other tips on keeping your interest up through long projects, see chapter 8, "Constructing Your Piece."

## IS IT WORTH MAKING?

Just because you can make a project doesn't mean you *should*. Before embarking on construction, think about whether the project is worthwhile. Go back to your *Why*, your reason for making the piece. Will the piece serve your purpose? Is the cost within your budget? And is it the best possible use for your creative time right now? Life is short; if this project isn't at the top of your list, and you haven't committed it to someone, work on what draws you more.

# CONSTRUCTING YOUR PIECE

Once you've completed enough of your design to begin building, take a few minutes to think through making the piece—at least, as much of it as you've designed in advance. Thinking through the steps in construction will help you identify and plan for difficult parts, and prevent you from painting yourself into a corner later. If you are new to a craft, you will likely want to work out the construction step by step; once you're more familiar with your tools and materials, you can step through faster until the whole process becomes nearly unconscious.

While the exact details of construction are unique to every piece, some strategies will make developing your piece simpler and less risky. Not all of these strategies are applicable to each piece, so apply only those that work well with your design and medium.

## ROUGH OUT THE ENTIRE PIECE
## BEFORE COMMITTING TO DETAILS

Starting with broad strokes means roughing out the big parts of the piece before moving on to finishing details. You don't need to put all the parts together, but you should make sure they will fit together into a coherent whole before adding finishing touches. Making sure the parts go together gracefully ensures that your details will merge harmoniously with the rest of the piece. Roughing out the design in the beginning also means you can fix the big design issues relatively cheaply, since you haven't invested any time in building out details yet.

A good example comes from fine arts. When an artist is drawing something—a face, perhaps—the very first act is to loosely sketch the entire face. The artist sets out the location, proportions, and size of each feature before developing the details. Details are usually developed over the entire piece—the artist partially develops one part, then moves on to another, and saves the finishing details for the very end. In this way, he or she makes sure the piece fits together harmoniously, right down to the final details.

Usually I have a very clear vision of what I want. Sometimes I don't bother to do a drawing because I know exactly what I want, so I just go ahead and make it.

But often, when I'm painting, I'll draw it because I want to see it, visually, to know if I'm satisfied before I start painting. So, because I paint on glass, often I do a full-scale drawing. Sometimes I'll even color it in with chalk pastels, because I love chalk pastels.

Then I'll just lay the sheet of glass on top of it and then I know what I want to do with the paint. I paint very wet, so I cover the drawing almost immediately. I've already seen it full scale, and know the color I'm thinking of works and so I can go ahead and paint because I already have a visual reference for what I want.

*Paul Marioni, glass artist*

Paul Marioni. *ALBINO JAGUAR*, 2002. Pastel on paper. 26" × 23".

Paul Marioni. *ALBINO JAGUAR*, 2002. Enamels fired on glass. 26" × 23". *Photographer: Russell Johnson.*

## GET FEEDBACK

As you develop the piece, get feedback on your design and construction. Show it to fellow artists, potential customers, or your client if you have one. (Chapter 11, "Celebrations and Contemplations," has some suggestions for getting feedback from others.)

If you are building prototypes, try using the prototype in its intended environment to get an idea of how well it functions. To learn even more, ask others to use it. They will find flaws (and strengths) that may surprise you.

Mea Rhee. *Textured Jars with Wire Handles*, 2015. Wheel-thrown stoneware with nichrome wire handles. 5" × 5.5" × 5". *Photographer: Mea Rhee.*

All of my work goes through a first draft, second draft, third draft, etc. So my design process takes months, or sometimes even longer, before an idea becomes an actual product. Most of the new ideas that I attempt in my studio don't end up in my final line of work. I go through and discard lots of ideas compared to the ones that I actually keep.

After every draft that I make, I often use the pots in my own kitchen for some period of time, just to make sure that they function the way that they're supposed to.

*Mea Rhee, potter*

## DESIGN TO MAKE CONSTRUCTION EASIER

If a portion of your design will be particularly hard to make, consider changing it. What are some cheaper possibilities?

What is your overall goal for the design? Can that be satisfied with a simpler design? This is particularly important if you are designing for production—a small savings in time can make a big difference to labor costs. And reworking an overly tricky section can be costly, too.

With the original size and shape of [my chopsticks bowl], I could fit five of them onto a kiln shelf while firing. There were awkward small spaces left over. There was a point where I changed the shape and size of the bowl slightly—one centimeter here, one centimeter there, in order to make use of that awkward leftover space. Now I can fit seven bowls tightly on one shelf, and it works out perfectly. That's something I always consider when designing pieces that I intend to make in lots of volume: "How does it fit into the kiln?"

Practicality and production efficiency are big factors for me.

*Mea Rhee, potter*

## FOCUS ON YOUR DESIGN GOALS; STAY FLEXIBLE

As you make construction choices, stay flexible by focusing on your overall goals, not specific details. Don't zoom in on an answer too quickly; instead, consider your goal and think up other possible solutions. Think about the characteristics you need in a material or a design, rather than a specific item.

## ANTICIPATE AND MANAGE RISKS

To reduce the risk of mistakes, think through the construction of the piece and identify places where you might run into trouble. Pay special attention to unfamiliar parts—tools, skills, materials, or processes you haven't used before. Those are usually the riskiest areas. Break those parts of the construction process down until you've found the problematic steps.

Once you've identified the likely problem areas, take a moment to identify the ones that will have the most impact on your project. The higher the likelihood of a mistake, and the more expensive the mistake, the more important it is to address it in advance.

There are basically two ways to reduce the potential negative impact of a risky part. The first is to reduce the likelihood of the mistake; the second is to decrease the cost of the mistake. So, for example, if you don't yet have the skills to complete a particularly tricky part, you could decrease the odds of the mistake by practicing that skill beforehand. Or you could reduce the cost of the mistake by making that part separate from the rest of the project. That way, if disaster strikes, you only have to redo one part—not the entire piece.

If you can't make the risky part separately, another way to reduce the impact of an error is to do the troublesome part as early in the project as possible. The less you have invested in the project, the less there is to lose should something go wrong.

Finally, consider redesigning to eliminate the difficult part, especially if you are doing production work. Time and materials lost to mistakes eventually means lost money.

If there's a design that creates a tricky problem every time I make it, I stop making it. As a production potter, you have to be fast. So if something is causing you a regular problem in production, you have to stop making it.

*Mea Rhee, potter*

Detail of Tien Chiu's *Autumn Splendor*. Photographer: Joe Decker.

# EXAMPLE: *AUTUMN SPLENDOR*

Here's an example that ties some of these ideas together.

As I was finishing my handwoven coat *Autumn Splendor*, I wanted to decorate the top with leaf motifs. The leaves would decorate the top part of the piece (which I felt looked too plain); place the focal point near the wearer's face, to draw attention there; and help move the eye through the piece by offering a series of design elements to move the eye along the curve. I also wanted to emphasize the autumn theme by adding large, visible leaves.

I planned to paint the leaves directly onto the fabric, giving the impression of leaves drifting in the wind. But when I did my risk analysis, mentally walking through the construction steps, I realized that the odds of a major mistake were just too high. My painting skills were quite limited, and an error would have been catastrophic—I had already invested hundreds of hours in weaving the cloth and sewing the garment. Because painting is irreversible, I would have only one chance to get the design right. That made the painting step fraught with risk.

I considered my options. I could reduce the risk by developing my painting skills, but that would have cost many hours of practice. And it still wouldn't address the inflexibility of a painted design.

Because the risk of painting the leaves wrong was unacceptably high, I chose to reduce the risk by making the leaves separately. I decided to paint the leaves on a different piece of cloth, then attach them to the garment. That way, if I made a mistake, I'd only have to redo one leaf—not the entire garment. It wasn't what I had intended, but because I was staying focused on my design goals and not clinging tightly to my original plan, I knew I could make the change and still be satisfied.

As I started construction, though, I realized that painting the leaves was still going to be a lot of effort, because my skills weren't up to the task. So I redesigned to simplify construction, using embroidery rather than painting, so I could take advantage of my much stronger embroidery skills. The resulting leaves came out beautifully, and much stronger, design-wise, than my original idea of painting the leaves directly onto the fabric.

# LARGE PROJECTS

Large projects pose some unique challenges, especially if they are time-consuming and repetitive. To sustain your interest over a piece that can span several months, consider some of these options.

Start by breaking down a big project into a series of smaller goals. If you are making a large piece that will take months, set yourself a goal of finishing a certain amount per week. If you find you can't finish that much, set yourself a smaller goal until you arrive at something achievable. Breaking down a big project into more manageable chunks helps maintain a sense of progress. Particularly for large projects, progress on the overall project may seem glacial, but if you are making good progress on smaller chunks, it's easier to keep yourself motivated.

Next, set objectives specifically for each section. How perfect can you make the next section? Or, how quickly can you make it?

Consider ways to vary your tasks. Are there different types of work you can do in parallel? Adding some variety to your daily work will help you keep your energy up.

Think also about what you can learn during the project. It's easier to sustain interest over long projects if they incorporate some new ideas or require you to learn new skills. Applying the same, familiar techniques for months at a time can become boring, but a novel technique can spark new interest.

Finally, practice kaizen. Kaizen is a concept from Japanese manufacturing practices, a process of making continual small improvements that add up to make a big difference. Think about your technique. Pay attention to what you're doing—strive for smoother motions, better ergonomics, greater efficiency. This makes an otherwise boring pursuit into something calling for rapt attention. You'll keep yourself engaged, and you'll grow a lot.

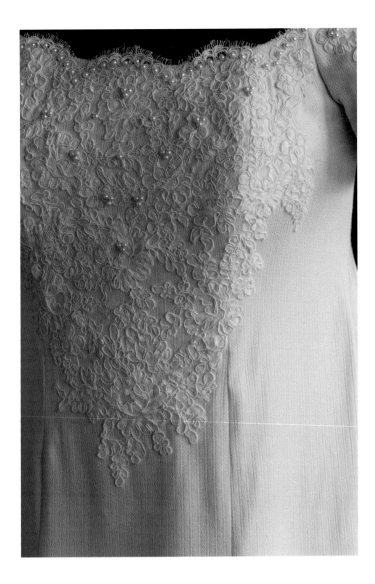

Tien Chiu. *Eternal Love Wedding Ensemble* (dress), 2010. Handwoven wedding dress in silk thread, Alençon lace, and pearls. *Photographer: Joe Decker.*

# EXAMPLE: WEDDING DRESS

For my marriage ceremony, I decided to make a handwoven, couture-sewn wedding dress. I didn't want the engagement to drag on forever, so I decided to limit the project to twelve months. I consulted with more experienced weavers and seamstresses, and concluded that, given the time I had available, it would probably take five months to weave the fabric and seven months to sew the dress using couture techniques (which require considerably more time than "regular" sewing).

I considered what it would take to weave the cloth. I would have to weave sixteen yards of fine silk for the dress, and another sixteen yards for the coat I planned to wear over the dress. I broke down my five-month estimate into the major steps: It would probably take about four weeks to weave the samples and six weeks to weave each batch of cloth. (I left the remaining month as insurance against disasters.)

Tien Chiu. *Eternal Love Wedding Ensemble* (coat), 2010. Handwoven wedding coat in silk, wool, and metallic gold thread. *Photographer: Joe Decker.*

I knew I didn't have the focus to do nothing but weave for four months—I'd get bored and drop the project. So I looked for tasks I could do in parallel. It turned out that I could perfect the dress design—sewing mockup after mockup—while weaving the cloth. By doing so, I added variety to my work. When I got bored with weaving, I could work on the dress design; when I got tired of working on the dress, I could go weave. And because I was completely unfamiliar with fashion design, the dress mockups meant I would be learning something new.

Even with that, I needed help sustaining interest in the weaving, which (once everything is set up) is an extremely repetitive task. So I decided to break down each sixteen-yard length of fabric into one-yard chunks. I made a sheet with sixteen boxes, and every time I completed a yard of fabric, I'd check off one box. This might have seemed silly to an outsider, but it reassured me that I was making progress.

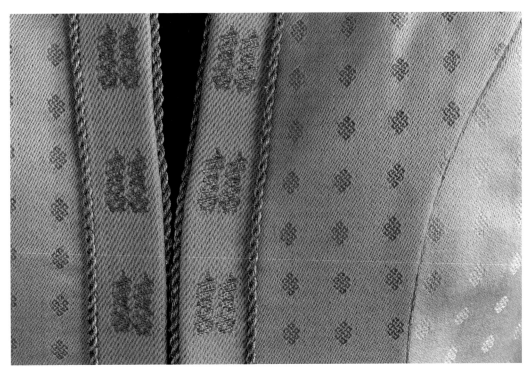

Detail of *Eternal Love Wedding Ensemble* (coat). *Photographer: Joe Decker.*

I also decided to practice kaizen, to make each yard of cloth go faster. Was there a more efficient way of weaving? Could I make more fluid motions, speed things up, make fewer errors? I did some research on the Web and discovered better ways to hold and use my weaving tools. Practicing the new methods made the weaving fly by faster. I actually felt a little disappointed when the weaving was finally done.

I used similar techniques during the sewing of the garment—trying new things and practicing skills throughout the construction. The result? A beautiful wedding dress and wedding coat, and a project that engaged me through an entire year of work. I got many compliments at my marriage ceremony, and both dress and coat are now part of the permanent collection at the American Textile History Museum. But I could never have finished them without using these methods for large projects.

# EVALUATING YOUR WORK-IN-PROGRESS

Evaluating your work frequently during the design and construction process is an essential part of the Creative Cycle. It enables you to identify and correct flaws quickly, strengthening the piece and making mistakes cheaper to correct.

Here are some suggestions for how to evaluate your work.

## START WITH *WHO* AND *WHY*

To evaluate a partially designed or constructed piece, start with your vision, your *Who* and *Why* for the work. Will the piece appeal to the person it's intended to please? Does the design fill the needs expressed in *Why*?

Starting with *Who* and *Why* makes sure both that you are meeting your goals and that you are not locking yourself into tunnel vision when designing a piece. It's easy to attach so firmly to your original intent for a design—the *What* of your piece—that you miss other solutions to the design goals embodied in *Why*.

Once you've revisited *Who* and *Why*, you're ready to move on to *What*.

## EVALUATE *WHAT*

Evaluating *What* is basically a matter of looking at the design and construction of a piece. After you're confident that the design satisfies *Who* and *Why*, consider how well your design will function in its intended use. Review chapter 4, "Functional Design," for things to consider.

Once you're satisfied with the functional design, consider the visual design. Read through chapter 5, "Visual Design," and think through the context and message of the piece. Does the piece work harmoniously with its planned context, and convey the mood or message that you want?

Think also about the visual story told by the piece. What do you want the viewer to pay attention to first? How are you guiding the viewer's eye through the piece? If your design is not telling an effective visual story, note that down so you can address it in the next step of the Creative Cycle, Change.

This is a great time to get feedback from other people—especially customers. Use the suggestions in chapter 11, "Celebrations and Contemplations," to get the most out of your feedback sessions.

If you have started making your piece, look at the quality of its construction. If you are throwing a pot, is it symmetrical, or is it unintentionally lopsided? If you are finishing wood, is the finish even, or full of drips and blotches? Consider whether the construction meets your quality bar for this particular piece.

When evaluating construction, don't rip the piece apart looking for errors. That way lies madness, as even great work has lots of flaws if you look closely enough. Instead, restrict yourself to looking for serious mistakes. Then consider what quality level you need. If you are making a casual piece for yourself, a few minor construction errors won't be fatal. But if you are planning to enter the piece in competition, the bar for technical quality needs to be higher. In that case, you may want to consider fixing or redoing a mistake.

Finally, evaluate the practicality of your design. Do you have the skills, tools, and materials to make your design? Do you have the time and attention span needed to complete it? And does it fit within your budget? Review chapter 7, "Practical Considerations," for things to think about.

# EVALUATION PRINCIPLES

Perfectionism is a common pitfall during the Evaluate phase of the Creative Cycle. It's easy to focus on all the things that are not yet right. But don't give up in frustration. Finding and fixing what's wrong—and building on what works well—is a big part of the Creative Cycle.

The guidelines below will help you evaluate your work without falling prey to perfectionism.

## Build on positives

Start your evaluation by focusing on the good parts. What's working for you? What do you really like? What are the essential elements of the piece?

This isn't a matter of being nice before launching into negative thoughts. The most important part of evaluating a project, particularly early on, is figuring out what is working—what you want to emphasize and build upon. You won't get a brilliant piece by trying to subtract everything you hate. Instead, start with the good points and make them better. Then fix the weaker points. You'll get a much stronger piece that way.

So start with the things you love and work with them first. It's not just good for you—it's good for your art.

Some days, especially when working with natural dyes, a color just isn't feeling like doing it. And I'm not talking about stars lining up and stuff—it's just humidity, temperature, in some cases how much sleep I had. All of those things interact with each other, so when a piece is not working, I try to see what *is* working and let that be the piece. I wind up with livelier, happier pieces that I am happy to keep or to present to a client as my best work.

*John Marshall, surface design artist*

## Don't torture your work

Lots of artists, when asked to evaluate their work, will ruthlessly zoom in on everything that might possibly be wrong. This is not the way of kindness, either for yourself or your work. Working with a design is a bit like creating bonsai. You can't violently chop an adult tree into bits to make a tiny bonsai; you have to work with the tree while it's young, and patiently shape the tree a little bit at a time. While you might need to prune out some portions—including some large branches—of your work, remember that it's like a living creature, best coaxed into changing. There's no need to hack it apart.

## It doesn't have to be complete

You don't need a design for the piece to evaluate how it's going—just critique the elements you've decided on so far. For example, in this preliminary sketch of a garment, only the colors, shape, and a crude idea of décor have been determined. That's fine, since the purpose of the sketch is to test the overall design and shape. Evaluate just the elements you have—you'll fill in the details later.

Early concept sketch for artwear garment.

## It doesn't have to be perfect

Your work doesn't have to be perfect—either in the finished piece, or in the initial design.

Some artists will iterate endlessly on designs, not entirely satisfied with any design, never moving into the actual work. This usually arises from perfectionism, wanting the design to be "just so" before executing it.

The truth is that trying to perfect a design before making it never works. Invariably, unexpected things happen—maybe you get a brilliant idea halfway through the piece, or maybe one part of the design collapses to mush when you try to make it. The process of making something is fraught with chaos, and trying to clearly predict the entire finished piece in advance is simply not possible. Things change, and your design will change with it. No design is final until the piece is complete—and sometimes not even then. If you are working in series, you can simply carry the design idea over into the next piece.

When you're pondering whether to continue forward with a design, ask yourself whether it feels good enough to explore further. If so, keep developing it. If not, go back and improve it, or select another design. But it *doesn't* have to be good enough to commit to a final piece—just enough to move one step further along in the process. Your designs will likely evolve continuously from the first brainstormed thoughts to the final lick of work—they're never perfect, never finished. But designs don't have to be perfect to produce good work. They just need to be good enough for the next step.

# EXERCISE 5: EVALUATING YOUR WORK-IN-PROGRESS

1. Examine what you've done so far on the project you're currently working on. Write down what you like most about it. This is the foundation, the thing you'll build on.

2. Think of ways to strengthen the things you like. Consider how the rest of the piece can support the aspects that please you. For example, if you like a particular shade of blue, adding a touch of a complementary color—perhaps a dull orange or brown—will make the blue appear brighter and more prominent. Or if you like the style of a particular part, how can you bring that pizzazz into the rest of the piece?

3. Once you've thought of ways to enhance the aspects you like, look closely at the rest of the piece. What parts of your design will work with your proposed changes? What won't work?

4. Alter the design (or the work-in-progress) to eliminate the distractions and the parts that don't work.

5. Evaluate the new design against the criteria set up in the first two sections of this chapter. Check to make sure that the functional design and visual design still work well, and that it meets the *Why* of the piece.

6. Start making your improved design!

# 10

# EVOLVING YOUR DESIGN

Once you've evaluated your piece, you'll need to decide whether and how to change the design. Perhaps you don't like the way the design is progressing, or you made a mistake in construction. Maybe you came up with a great new idea that requires revisiting the entire design.

## FIND OUT WHAT TROUBLES YOU

The first step in identifying what needs to change is to ask yourself what is bothering you. Sometimes it's obvious: "Oops! I made that cut deeper than I intended." But design problems can be more elusive. Sometimes you can feel, intuitively, that something is wrong, but can't immediately identify what. In those cases, putting it aside for a few days, or putting it somewhere where you'll run across it unexpectedly, can help.

Really study it. Try to get a different bead on it. Maybe put it upside down in the garden and get up on the roof to look at it. Put it somewhere where you're going to catch it unexpectedly. You know, as you enter the house, or in the hall, on the wall. Something like that. You're going to catch it, and you're going to suddenly see "Oh God! What it needs is . . . "

If that doesn't happen, if I know there's something wrong and I can't analyze it, I'll just start changing some of the elements of it. Maybe that yellow is just too bright. So I'll cut a more mustardy piece of fabric and pin it up there to damp down the yellow. Or maybe [a pink] should be a brighter pink or there should be more contrast here and less there, etc.

You just play with elements. That's how I troubleshoot, really.

*Kaffe Fassett, knitter, needlepoint designer, and quilter*

# GO BACK TO YOUR VISION

Once you understand what's bothering you about the piece, go back to *Why* and *What*. How is the problematic section clashing with your objectives for the piece? Is it actually clashing at all?

You have to think about your vision. You have to clarify your vision—clarify what you want, because if you don't accomplish it, you're not going to be satisfied. You may even give up or do something else. So focus on your vision, and don't worry about what other people think. You're the only one that knows what you want to do or accomplish with this artwork.

*Paul Marioni, glass artist*

Paul Marioni. *FLASH*, 2011. Kinetic cast glass, mirrored. 19" × 14" × 5". *Photographer: Russell Johnson.*

Making a successful piece doesn't require it work out the way you intended. Instead, consider how to accomplish your personal goals in making the piece, and how to make it useful to the end user. It's easy to get so focused on your intent for a particular section that you lose track of other ways to succeed. Checking your original *Why* for the piece, and seeing whether there really is a conflict, helps you remember that there may be other solutions.

## BRAINSTORM WAYS TO MAKE IT MEET YOUR GOALS

Once you've put your finger on what needs to be fixed and why, don't jump at the first solution. Take some time and think of other ways to solve the problem. Often the first few ideas won't be as good as later ones, so investing a few more minutes to think of alternatives is usually worthwhile.

The first thing I learned—the hard way—is not to flail. Don't jump in and do something in a hurry, without thinking it through.

If something is really not working, only rarely will I just pick up a new screen and print over it or wad it up and throw it in a dye bath. That's the first thing I used to do, and it almost always failed.

I'm a lot bigger now on walking away from something and thinking I need a little time. It's no different from having an argument with another person. When you're in the heat of the argument you're almost always going to say something that you'll regret later. So it's always better to walk away and cool off.

I feel the same way about my work. Of course it isn't alive, but if I'm in the studio and it's giving me fits, rather than argue with it and wrestle it to the ground, it's better for me to walk away and develop a strategy for what might work next.

And when I do that, I make what I call my "elegant" list. After I've calmed down, I look at a piece and think "Okay, I could do this, or I could do this, or I could do that, or I could . . . " I brainstorm as many possibilities as I can think of for how to change it or resurrect it. And then I have something to work with, because it isn't just doing the first thing that pops into my head. It isn't doing the first one-trick-pony thing that usually saves something. Brainstorming many possibilities allows me to respond to what's happening. I can think, "Well, these top three ideas are crap, that's not going anywhere. But the fourth and fifth ideas—one of those might really work."

And then I might tentatively explore one of those ideas, resolving the piece. Nine times out of ten, the piece gets stronger. But it does take that incubation time—thinking about what to do next, not just rushing through.

*Jane Dunnewold, surface design artist*

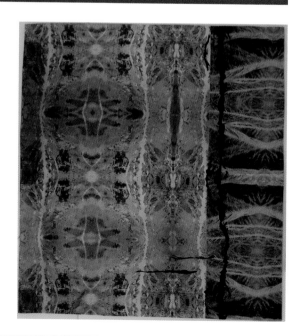

Jane Dunnewold. *Feather Study 2*, 2014.
Digitally printed fabric from a photo of a feather
as viewed under a microscope, assembled,
backed, and machine quilted. 60" × 65".
*Photographer: Jane Dunnewold.*

# CHOOSE AN APPROACH TO WORK WITH

Once you've brainstormed some choices, you'll want to evaluate them to see which one you want to implement. Here are some things to think about as you make your choice:

The first criterion for any change is whether it will help accomplish your *Why* for the piece. However, the approach that gets you closest to your original vision may not be the best overall approach. Consider the cost of each solution, in time, materials, and effort. A choice might be effective but way too costly, especially if the piece is intended for sale.

Consider risk as well. How likely is your solution to go awry, and how bad will it be if it does? Are you willing to run that risk to get the benefits of that approach?

# MANY PATHS TO HAPPINESS

As you evaluate your ideas, keep in mind that there are many routes to meeting your design goals. It's easy to obsess over finding the best way to fix the problem, but many times you have lots of equally good options, and it simply comes down to personal preference and your whim of the moment. If you really can't decide among options, it generally means that any of them will work just fine, so just choose one and keep going. You don't have to figure out the One True Way.

I had a student once who literally threw her body over the work we were mocking up on the table, because I kept saying, "Let's try it this way, let's try it that way, let's try it this way." I was trying to prove to her that there was no right or wrong, that there were more possibilities. She got mad at me and threw her body across the work table and said, "Stop! You're ruining it!" And with that she walked out of the class. But she came back in about half an hour later, and she said, "I learned such a valuable lesson. It really doesn't matter. There are many ways to solve the problem."

What I was trying to do was show her that there was more than one way it would work. She was so frightened to make her own decision, and once she realized that she could make that decision she was very successful. And we're still friends.

*Yvonne Porcella, quilter*

Yvonne Porcella. *Wonderland*, 2012. Silk and cotton. 60" × 42".
*Photographer: Cathie I. Hoover.*

## DON'T HESITATE TO CHANGE YOUR DESIGN

Often the best solution isn't to alter the piece to conform to your planned design, but to change your design to accommodate—or even exploit—the problem. Some Japanese artisans, when faced with a broken vessel that is precious to them, will add gold to highlight the crack when mending it. This turns what would otherwise be a flaw—a visible crack in the bowl—into beauty.

I designed [Berroco's "Dickson" skirt] as a poncho. It came in from the knitter and it looked a little bit loose, but it looked like a poncho until I steamed it and loosened up the rib even more. Then I put it on the dress form. It started sliding down, and it just slid down the dress form, past the waist, until it hit the hip of the dress form and stopped.

Three or four of us in the office were there watching this and I said, "Okay, it wants to be a skirt." And it became a skirt. And it became the most popular pattern in the book.

*Norah Gaughan, knitwear designer*

Norah Gaughan. *Dickson*, 2013. Skirt knitted from alpaca yarn. © *Berroco, Inc.*

John Marshall. *Galactic Warrior*, 1979. Tsutsugaki (cone-applied paste resist) over silk noil, chicken wire, maegane, jade, coral, papier-mâché, gold leaf, natural pigments. Size medium.

I was working on a piece with a Chinese-style cloud collar, and I wanted it to have a skirt with a similar shape. Well, the dyeing went exactly as I wanted. It came together exactly as I wanted, but when I put it together it looked so dorky I couldn't stand it.

So I took the skirt, put chicken wire behind it, turned it upside down, and it became a helmet.

That was a situation where everything worked, but it was not a happy piece. It cooperated with me, I cooperated with it, it was exactly what I wanted, but it looked stupid! So I had to allow for that, write off my ego tied up with the original design, and re-adjust so that I could be happy with it in a new way. That was by turning it upside down and not forcing it to stay as I had intended it.

*John Marshall, surface design artist*

There's no such thing as a mistake. I taught myself weaving, and used yarns that I thought I loved, not knowing that they would catch on the beater and would break. I had a terrible time. But what I did was embroider over the breaks. And I won a ribbon on that piece.

So I show my students that. It's not a mistake, you just have to look at it a different way.

*Yvonne Porcella, quilter*

Yvonne Porcella. *Handwoven and Embroidered Skirt*, 1964. Linen, wool, mohair, silk, cotton. 35" × 20". *Photographer: Yvonne Porcella*.

# EXERCISE 6: MAKING AN ACTION PLAN FOR DESIGN CHANGE

1. Take a piece that isn't working for you. Consider its better points and its flaws. If you haven't already, consider doing the "Evaluating your work-in-progress" exercise in chapter 9 to help identify what's working and what's not.

2. Brainstorm a list of ways to strengthen the piece. Think about (but don't limit yourself to) the following options as you brainstorm:

   a. Strengthen the parts that work, drawing attention to the better parts and away from the parts that don't.

   b. Incorporate the flaws into the design. A wise teacher once told me, "A flaw that appears once or twice looks like a mistake. Three times becomes a design element."

   c. Make the flaws beautiful. (I once fixed the too-short underskirt of a dress by adding a gorgeous piece of lace at the bottom. The result looked better than my original intent, and no one was the wiser.)

   d. Add design elements to cover up whatever isn't working.

   e. Let go of your initial vision. Will the piece work well if used a different way, or with a different theme?

3. Go down your list. Evaluate each possibility: How much stronger will it make the piece? How much will it cost to put into practice? Is there a better solution?

4. Choose one possibility to work with. If you're feeling tentative about your solution, do an experiment or create a sample to see whether it works. If you feel more confident about it, just dive in and do it.

---

# IF IT ISN'T WORKING

What if it really isn't working for you? There are a few possibilities. One is simply to put the piece away for a while, so you can see it with fresh eyes. It's easy to get frustrated with something because it didn't conform to your vision, but if you set your original vision aside, fresh possibilities may spring up. Or stash it away in a reject bin for a while—even if the piece didn't work, you may find possibilities for other projects arising from an unsuccessful piece.

One of the most liberating realizations I had as an artist was that I could discard things. I don't throw a lot of stuff away. I have a big pitch bin and I pitch stuff that isn't working into it. Periodically, I go back to it and I'll look at it and I'll say, "Hmm, yes, well, that was an interesting idea but it didn't translate well, or I didn't do this well, or I didn't do that well."

But maybe I'll revisit it.

*Rachel Carren, polymer artist*

---

Another alternative is to get rid of the piece entirely. If you're obsessing over it or if it's become mental clutter, get it out of your life. Swap it for another artist's piece of work, donate it to a charity, or just throw it away.

I don't have any problem now with just abandoning something that wasn't working, or cutting it up. Or taking it over to Goodwill, figuring somebody is going to discover this and think, "Hot dog, man, I know what I can do with that right now!"

And then I'm happy because I don't want to clutter up my studio with things that haven't worked.

*Jane Dunnewold, surface design artist*

If something is not working, I will destroy it and start over. In felting, once it's done, there's not a whole lot you can do to alter it. I like to have a clean slate in my studio, so if things aren't going well, I'll generally just destroy it. It doesn't happen very often.

*Andrea Graham, felter*

# CELEBRATIONS AND CONTEMPLATIONS

## RECOGNIZE WHEN YOU'RE DONE

First of all, how do you know when to wrap up work on your project and call it done (or "done enough")? On some pieces, it's obvious when you're done. On others, it's not so clear. If you're satisfied with the visual and functional design, and you think the construction is sound, you're done. If there's something you're not happy with, Exercise 6 will help you evaluate whether it's worth changing, and decide how to change it. Consider the questions in Exercise 6, to be sure you're at the endpoint that's right.

Notice that you don't have to be 100% satisfied with a project to consider it done. Very few of my projects completely satisfy me, and that, to my mind, is wonderful. It means I am still growing as an artist. Further, the deficiencies in my current project often inspire me with ideas for the next project. They are like trail markers, pointing out directions for my future work.

## CELEBRATE THE COMPLETION

Once you decide you're done, it's time to celebrate! It's a simple way to reward and encourage your creative spirit. For small projects, go for a walk, have a cold beer, or soak in a hot bath—do something you enjoy but don't do often enough. For big projects? Drink some champagne. Celebrate with friends, take that trip you've been wanting to do—something to mark it as a special occasion.

Why emphasize celebration? In the thick of a project, it's often easy to focus on the things that went wrong, or the things you wish you could have done better. Stepping back for a moment and celebrating the finish helps you honor the things that went right. Even if the project didn't turn out entirely as you liked, there will be portions that you think are great, or that you really enjoyed making. Celebrate those aspects. And honor your efforts as well. You worked in your craft, you learned from the process, and you grew your skills in design and craft. That's worth a celebration!

## REFLECT ON GOALS

To decide whether your project was a success, you'll want to go back to your goals for the piece—the *Why*, *What*, and *How*.

### Reflect on Why

To reflect on *Why*, go back to your original goals for the project. Did you set out to learn something, or try a new process? Did you want to make a gift for someone, or produce a piece that would sell?

If you achieved your personal goals for the project, then the project was successful—even if the finished piece doesn't match your expectations.

Pay close attention to how you grew during the project. Did you learn something new? Did you stretch your design and construction skills, and if so, where? Particularly if you are frustrated with the piece, it's important to recognize and celebrate your growth during the process of making it.

Conversely, if you learned nothing during this project, ask yourself whether you can take on something more challenging next time. Creative work is most fun when you're exploring and learning, and sticking to the familiar doesn't build your skills or sharpen your eye.

[In traditional woodworking using hand tools], the feedback from the environment and from the materials is more present and open. You can actually feel the wood.

A big part of the craftsmanship is working in an emergent process. Each piece is built with an eye towards what you did before. You build a chair, and rather than saying, "Here, I've made all the pieces, let's put it together," you put together one sub-assembly and then fit the next pieces to that, however that ended up. So it is an emergent process. But even on a micro level, it's also emergent in that with every stroke of the plane, every cut of the saw, you're responding and building upon the piece. You get the feedback from each stroke, and correct the material.

If you don't learn from the sound and the feedback and the response, then you can't do it right. And on the larger time scale of finishing a project, again, if you don't learn from it and change accordingly, then it has not been very useful for you.

*Roy Underhill, woodworker*

Roy Underhill
at work.
*Photographer:*
*Roy Underhill.*

## Reflect on How

To reflect on your process, start by paying attention to what you liked and didn't like about designing and making the piece. How can you do more of the things you liked? If there are techniques you particularly enjoyed, consider adding them to future projects. If you continue to develop them, they may become part of your creative voice.

For things you didn't enjoy, think of ways to make them less frustrating. Do you need to acquire technical skills? Design skills? If you got bored halfway through a step, think of ways to make it more interesting, or else learn how to speed it up.

I really pay attention to the process more than the finished piece. I think, "Okay, I want to hammer out some metal and see what comes out." So I might make a piece and say, "Well, that really felt good. And it looked okay." So, the process might get high marks, the end result might get a B minus. And that's okay with me.

*Tim McCreight, metalworker*

Now, think back . . . when were you having fun? When were you frustrated? Make a list of the particularly memorable steps, and ask yourself why each stood out. Then think about how to multiply the good moments in future projects, and how to minimize the bad ones. Look particularly for themes—areas where you were consistently frustrated, or areas where a lot of good stuff happened.

Don't limit yourself to making only large changes. Continual small improvements add up to a big impact. If you continually improve your process, making both large and small changes, you'll soon find yourself with a more efficient, effective, and enjoyable process for creating new work.

# EXERCISE 7: IMPROVING YOUR PROCESS

1. Make a list of all the steps in designing and making the project.

2. Pick out several steps that you particularly enjoyed and several steps that you found frustrating, boring, or otherwise distasteful.

3. For the steps that you enjoyed, write down why you enjoyed them. Are there ways to bring the things you liked into your next project?

4. For the steps you found less enjoyable, write down why you didn't like them. Brainstorm several ways to make each step more enjoyable in future projects, or to eliminate a step entirely.

5. If efficiency matters to you, look at the steps that take the longest time to complete. Brainstorm several ways to make that step faster or more efficient.

6. If meeting deadlines is important to you, look at the steps that you time-estimated poorly. Put the estimate and the actual time in your project notes, so you can improve your estimates later.

7. Write down your accomplishments during the design and construction of the piece. Did you learn something new? What milestones did you achieve?

This exercise may surprise you. Even if the final piece is not to your liking, if you've challenged yourself along the way, and enjoyed the process of making it, you've succeeded. And you may find that you've accomplished some astonishing things, even if the piece itself isn't what you dreamed it would be.

---

## Reflect on What: Evaluate your piece

After you're done reflecting on your goals and your process, evaluate the project itself, using the guidelines in Chapter 9 to assess the visual design, the functional design, and the construction. Get feedback from others, using the guidelines that appear later in this chapter. But don't obsess over what's right or what's wrong with the finished piece. Instead, focus on what you can take into the next piece. Your goal now is learning, not improving the completed piece.

If person A made a piece of jewelry, and person B says, "Gee, this line is a little cockeyed here, it bugs me, my eye keeps going to this wavy line. It's supposed to be straight. I just wish it was really straight." And then person A, the maker, says, "Yes, my file is dull, and my bench was wobbly and so I couldn't get a straight line." That's not the point. That might be entirely accurate, but that's not the point. The observation was a visual one, and valuable. If you're going to make a line straight, make it really straight. If it's going to be wobbly, make it really wobbly. That's good transferable information that you can carry to the next design.

The fact that this particular line is wobbly because of external reasons is really kind of pointless. Who cares? We're not talking about this piece, really. We're talking about the next piece. That's the one the critique is all about—the future, not the past or present.

*Tim McCreight, metalworker*

---

I believe that if you don't critique your own work, and the work of others, that you're not thinking. If you simply splash paint on the surface and consider yourself done, it doesn't matter. If there's no thought associated with it—about the process, the result, or the experience—then there's nothing learned. And if there's nothing learned, there's no point doing it in the first place.

*John Marshall, surface design artist*

John Marshall. *Indigo Clamp Resist*, 2012. Kyoukechi (compound clamp resist) over Japanese cotton, natural dyes. 14" × 36".

Here's a quick recap of things to consider.

Start with the aesthetic design of the piece. Review chapter 5, "Visual Design." Think about whether it fits with its environment, and whether it works well as the diva or as the supporting cast. Consider its visual story—where does your eye enter, where does it exit, and what does it see along the way?

Next, consider the functional design, as laid out in chapter 4, "Functional Design." Will the piece meet the uses laid out in Why?

Consider the practical aspects of the design, laid out in chapter 7, "Practical Considerations." Did you meet your budget, if you had one? If not, figure out what caused your costs to balloon, so you can fix it next time.

Similarly, if you were working to a deadline and missed it, or had to work in a panic towards the end, don't get frustrated. Just figure out how not to miss the next one—you may need to pad your estimates a bit more, or predict your work habits better. Don't flog yourself, just fix it.

Now—imperfections aside—do you like the piece? If so, you've succeeded, even if there are flaws.

Finally, consider the technical quality, the workmanship of the piece. Does it meet your intent for that particular piece? A piece need not be technically perfect to be a success. It just needs to be as good as you intended it to be. If you are making chainsaw sculpture, the rough-hewn nature of the piece is not a defect—it's just the nature of the piece.

Be honest with yourself. Acknowledge when you haven't met the standard you were striving for. Passing over your mistakes prevents you from correcting them.

Again, don't spend time dwelling on the finished piece. Instead, simply note its strengths and weaknesses, and how you would fix them in future work. Your evaluation isn't about this piece—it's about improving the next one.

If you're just learning how to be an acrobat and you fall over, you can't say, "That was intentional!" to justify it, as some people do. It's a lack of skill and experience.

*Rachel Carren, polymer artist*

A really good work is like a kiss from somebody that you can't forget!

*Kaffe Fassett, knitter, needlepoint designer, and quilter*

A collection of work by Kaffe Fassett. © Debbie Patterson.

While your vision is important while you're making the piece, you need to let go of it when you're done. You need to be able to evaluate the piece as it is, not as you intended it to be. It may well have evolved away from your original plan, and that's fine. Letting go of your original vision can be essential to seeing your completed work.

There are always things that are just not right. This isn't right, that isn't right. I found that rather than fight with it, the best thing is to just put it away. I think I'm starting to have short-term memory problems, and that's good because I don't remember what the problem was when I pull it out! I'm serious!

I have things that are twenty years old. I'll pull them out and think "Damn, that's pretty good!" And I have no idea what the problem was at the time. Well, the problem at the time was it wasn't going where I wanted it to go. And now when I look at it, I'm addressing it as it is. And so now, with maturity, or the forgetfulness of old age—whichever you want to call it—I can allow it to be what it is and work with that.

*John Marshall, surface design artist*

---

In a wood-fired pot, there are many changes in the overall surface [during firing]. Some parts of the kiln get more ash, and it melts. Some parts are a little bit cooler, and so come out different from the rest of the kiln. So each piece is unique. There are many different things that happen on the surface of the pot—at a certain temperature, the ash will start melting so you'll get drips on the side of your pot. A little further back where it isn't quite as hot, it might just be somewhat matte on the surface. Then further back it might have shades of brightness because the flame is going quite fast and there isn't a reduction atmosphere in that part of the kiln.

I have said before that if you can let go of your expectations and just accept whatever comes out, you'll be a lot happier on the day that we unload. Because we don't know what's going to happen. Each scenario is different. You can't just put a pot in the same spot two firings in a row and expect it to come out the same.

*Hiroshi Ogawa, ceramicist*

Hiroshi Ogawa. *Tea Bowl*. Wood-fired clay. 4" × 3.5" × 4". *Courtesy of Eutectic Gallery.*

You may find that you're too close to the piece to see it effectively. Many artisans prefer to wait weeks or months after a piece is complete to evaluate whether it was successful. Giving it a "cooling off" period helps you see it as it is, not as you intended it to be.

You put your stuff up and you stare at it a long time. You can converse with your offspring, as it were. I never put things away under a bed or in a closet. I put them on the wall, let them converse with me. I used to never let a painting be sold until I had adjusted it.

*Kaffe Fassett, knitter, needlepoint designer, and quilter*

Hiroshi Ogawa. *Rectangular Wall Platter*. Wood-fired clay. 14" × 11". *Courtesy of Eutectic Gallery*.

Sometimes they come out of the kiln and I grab my heart and just say "Ooh!" But I would say that doesn't happen a lot.

It's a slow process. I put it in my gallery room and I look at it over a period of weeks, and think what I might be able to do in the next firing to change different things as far as the neck or the form or something like that.

If I like it within a week or two after the opening, I think it was a success.

*Hiroshi Ogawa, ceramicist*

Because it can be hard to analyze your piece objectively, you may find it useful to do the exercise "Learning to see" from chapter 3, "Finding Inspiration." Look at your piece as if it were a strange object you just picked up, not something you just made. Look at the lines, shapes, and other design elements. Think about what you find appealing and what you don't. What ideas do you see embedded in the piece? Capture your discoveries in your inspirations notebook so you can use it in future projects.

As you're evaluating your pieces, it's critical to remember that *you are not your work*. As a practicing artisan, you will inevitably come across pieces that you feel were unsuccessful. But don't look at a poorly designed piece and think, "I'm no good." Every artist, including wildly successful and sophisticated ones, started out with poor quality work, and will continue to produce some unsuccessful pieces. A piece that doesn't work is simply a piece that doesn't work. It means you experimented with something that failed, and you need to understand why it failed so you can improve your next pieces. By learning from your mistakes, you can turn your failures into later success, strengthening yourself as an artist and improving your future body of work.

So a bad piece doesn't mean that you have no talent, or that you're not an artist. If you don't like your work, then figure out how to improve it. But don't decide you aren't an artist, and don't give up. You are not your work.

# GET INPUT FROM OTHERS

Once you've done your evaluation, consider asking others for their opinions. It's easy to get too close to your work to evaluate things objectively, particularly while you are making it. Getting input from others can help you decide whether a particular design aspect is working, or which direction will make a piece stronger. But to get good input, you need to provide some direction. (Otherwise you are likely to get "Well, I like it," which is pleasantly gratifying but not useful.)

If you can, try to find someone who's experienced in critiquing, especially for your first few feedback sessions. Getting feedback from an experienced critiquer will give you an idea of what to look for when seeking others' advice. It will also, of course, get you the best possible feedback for your work.

Here are some suggestions for getting the most from someone else's evaluation.

1. Be clear about what you want. Are you looking for feedback on your technical skills? Do you want the reviewer's perspective on the overall design? Are you wondering whether a particular part fits with the rest of the piece? There are millions of details in each piece, and asking specific questions helps your critiquer focus on the ones that matter to you. The more specific the question, the better focused the answer will be.

   However, beware of focusing too sharply: sometimes it's best to let the critiquer talk freely about what jumped out at him or her, rather than focusing on specific questions. It depends on the experience of the person doing the critique: experienced artists will know what to look for, while less experienced people need some guidance.

2. Ask open-ended questions. Don't settle for a yes or no answer, as they rarely provide useful information. Instead, ask questions that invite the reviewer to give you more information. For example, don't ask "Does this design work?" Instead, ask "What parts of this design work for you, and why?"

   If you really do want a yes or no answer, ask the reviewer to explain why he or she would answer yes or no. "Does the purple and yellow color combination in this piece work for you?" is a yes or no question, but can be made more informative by following up with "Why do you feel it is/isn't working?" or even "What can I do to improve the color scheme?"

3. Work with a critique group. A deep look at others' work is a great way to improve your own eye, and working with a small group gets you valuable feedback from multiple viewpoints. One of my guild's study groups meets once a month to discuss our pieces and works-in-progress, and to me it's the most valuable part of the guild.

   While it's great if you can find a critique group within your craft, your critique group does not have to work in your medium. In addition to my weaving group, I work with a critique partner whose medium is photography. He offers suggestions on my writing and my fiber arts projects; I offer feedback and ideas on his photos. It works very well for both of us—though neither of us has a deep understanding of the other's medium, good design is universal.

4. Opinions are opinions, not gospel. You are the one making your art. In fact, you are the only one who *can* make your art. In the end, it isn't about whether someone else (even a show judge) loves it or hates it; it's about whether you are personally satisfied with it. Other people can provide feedback and reactions to the piece, but remember—the only opinion that really matters is yours.

# WORKING IN SERIES

After reflecting, you may find that you want to develop some of the ideas in the piece a bit further. If so, bring them into the next piece. Working in series—developing a set of works exploring an idea or a theme—is a great way to develop your skills and your voice, since you can take what you learned from one piece into the next one, gradually refining your ideas.

Actually I don't see how you could get a lot of work done without working in series. Because you just can't invent new thought processes all the time.

I find it really rewarding because every time I think of a way to change something, I feel clever. It's really fun to think of something new that changes it, something that maybe hasn't been done before. You can perfect your thought process, explore deeper and get better, either more complicated or more beautifully simple if you're working in series.

*Norah Gaughan, knitwear designer*

I was intrigued by the ribbons of a drawing. It was a woman, from her back, sitting on the floor. I ended up making three tapestries of the same drawing, the same color, trying different things until I came to an understanding of what I might do. The fourth tapestry was bigger. The same pose, the same drawing, but bigger, different handling. But I needed to do the first few tapestries, you see, in order to reach the decisions [that I made in the final piece].

That's what I mean by an open journey.

*Archie Brennan, tapestry weaver*

## Artist's Statement, *Études*:

Études are musical studies employed by musicians to achieve mastery of an instrument. Through a series of conversations with a trumpet player friend, I realized that études are also a form of meditation. The potential exists for the playing to *center the player*. This explains why a player with a career spanning thirty years would continue to play études. The daily practice is its own reward.

I was surprised to recognize études as one more example of how individual meditation practices unfold. Some people sit zazen and Om every day. Others are part of a prayer circle. Musicians practice their instruments. As an artist, I achieve my daily centering in the studio.

Which is how this series of works was initiated. These forty-eight studies sprang from a four-month commitment to making/working every day as spiritual practice.

Selecting the color palette, the tools, and the materials prior to beginning encouraged discernment on the impact of limitations. Daily fuel for the practice emerged as a co-mingling of spiritual belief with a visual language crafted over twenty years. I was astonished and humbled by the breadth and richness of the imagery.

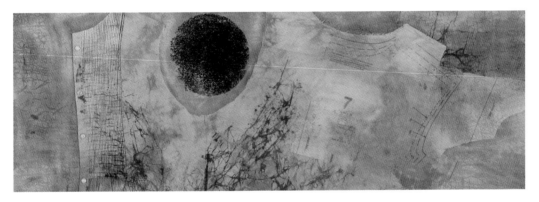

Jane Dunnewold. *Étude #13: Number 7: Open Heart*, 2011. Silk, ink, repurposed clothing, pattern paper, sand. 15" × 44". *Photographer: Jane Dunnewold.*

Jane Dunnewold. *Étude 24: Number 5: Choir*, 2011. Rice paper, felt, pattern paper, sand. 9.5" × 32". *Photographer: Jane Dunnewold.*

Jane Dunnewold. *Étude #36: Arabesque: Contemplation*, 2011. Silk, ink, repurposed clothing, sand. 11" × 44.5". *Photographer: Jane Dunnewold.*

Jane Dunnewold. *Étude #45: Intimate Rhythm: Larghetto*, 2011. Silk, felt, tuxedo shirt, dévoré. 11" × 44". *Photographer: Jane Dunnewold.*

And I experienced three revelations.

First, elements that had fallen into disuse over time re-asserted their meaning and became the perfect choice for a theme's resolution. I guess this makes sense. When we master spoken language, we don't abandon a word just because we've been using it a long time. So there was a palpable rightness to revising my symbolic visual repertoire.

Then, references to music and poetry crisscrossed the visual plane, bouncing against the imagery and firing into my unconscious, setting off fresh connections and moments of illumination. Those quirky, profound, new connections are the best thing about making. There is so much great stuff to think about.

And as the series evolved the visual surfaces simplified. I can only characterize this as a process of distillation. Are the last pieces of the series better or worse than those at the start? Or only different? That is probably a matter of personal opinion.

Because in the end, my real goal was to stay in present time. This disallows comparing one moment to another and hence, one piece to another. We are free to enjoy each of them on their own merits.

*Jane Dunnewold, surface design artist*

## SHARPENING YOUR SKILLS

So far we've discussed design and development of a single piece. But it's also important to think about yourself and your own creative development, over an entire body of work. What are your goals as an artisan? What skills do you want to develop, and how will you develop them? This chapter offers suggestions for improving the four basic skills: functional design, visual design, technical design, and construction. Functional design and visual design allow you to conceive your vision, technical design allows you to create the blueprints for it, and construction skills allow you to create it.

This chapter also contains suggestions for fine-tuning your creative process, making it more efficient and enjoyable.

## FUNCTIONAL DESIGN SKILLS

The best way to learn functional design is simply to observe. Take a critical look at the things you use daily. Are they easy to use? How could they be made better? You'd be surprised how many common objects are poorly designed—glass vases that fall over easily, ceramic teapots that dribble when pouring, drawers that can pull straight out, dropping their contents onto the floor.

Talk to people who use what you make. What works well for them? What doesn't? Watch them using your work if you can, to see for yourself what problems they may have. Use the piece yourself to see what you like and don't like about it. Write down your observations and work them into your next piece. The best way to learn is through observation and critique of the things around you.

# EXERCISE 8: EVALUATING SIMILAR PIECES

Go to a show or store that sells products similar to what you plan to make, and choose one to evaluate. The product need not be artisan made; mass-manufactured pieces are just as good for this exercise.

Use your chosen piece if you can—sit on a chair, try on jewelry, pick up a pitcher and try to pour from it. Take notes (mental if not physical) on what you like and dislike about the way it works.

In addition to your initial observations, think about the following areas:

**Utility:** Does it perform as expected? Is it the right size for your intended use? Is it easy to maintain?

**Ergonomics:** Is it comfortable to use? Can you imagine using it for long periods at a time?

**Longevity:** Does it need to last a long time? And if so, are the materials durable enough?

**Durability:** How tough is the piece? How do you expect it to meet its end?

Once you've evaluated the product and identified what works and what doesn't, brainstorm ways to improve the product's functionality. Follow the brainstorming rules outlined in chapter 6, "Getting Started." In particular, brainstorm lots of ideas, including really wild ones. Make sure your internal censor is turned off while brainstorming—otherwise you'll just come up with safe choices, not interesting ones. The goal of this exercise is to get yourself into the habit of thinking creatively about functional design. If you open up the way you think, you'll have succeeded, whether or not your designs are practical to make.

After you've gotten practice critiquing the work of others, do this exercise with your own work. While it's easier to analyze others' work objectively, eventually you will want to make sure that your own work meets the same standards. This means standing back and taking a critical look at your own functional designs.

# VISUAL DESIGN SKILLS

Craftspeople frequently approach visual design intuitively, through trial and error. But you can learn visual design much faster by taking classes. Design theory is part of the undergraduate curriculum in fine arts programs at the four-year college level, and also at community colleges. Many of these programs include classes in two-dimensional design, three-dimensional design, and color theory.

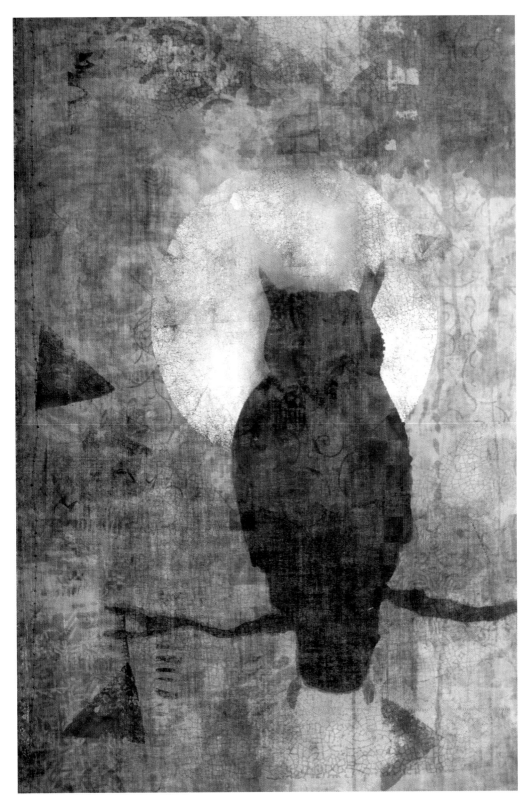

Jane Dunnewold. Detail of *Pilgrim*, 2005. Silk, cotton, gold leaf, pigment, dye, thread. 26" × 80". *Photographer: Jane Dunnewold.*

There's nothing like a good course [in design theory]. If you can take an online class, or even better, a real-time one—if you can get the assistance of somebody who has studied it and really understands it—that can help you cut to the chase.

There are some decent books you can work through, if that's the only option you have. But from the standpoint of figuring out balance, composition and all of that, you can struggle along for a long time when just a few tips from somebody who knows what they are doing would really help you.

I am self-taught, but I recognize that my own trajectory and development could have gone a lot faster if I had actually had the opportunity to take some classes instead of having to figure it all out on my own.

And definitely the same thing for color. Some people are intuitively good at choosing colors. I think that actually can work against you, because if you're intuitively good at putting colors together, you have such a high success rate that maybe you don't notice the times when it doesn't really work.

But I think once you've studied color, you really understand the principles, and you begin to see it in real time, then you know why you're putting certain things together and so it supports your intuitive ability in a way that reduces the number of failures even more.

While I used to be a little bit of a snob about classes and studying and course work and all that, I've come round to another way of thinking.

*Jane Dunnewold, surface design artist*

---

If classes in design theory aren't for you, you can pick up a lot of the same knowledge by reading through texts that cover the same material.

Once you understand the basic principles, it's critical to continue sharpening your eye. Look around you! Examine the natural world. Explore historical work in your craft. Go to shows and exhibits and study the pieces on display. Think constantly about what you like, what you don't like, and why. Write down what works for you, and what doesn't.

Critique is the most important thing. Because that's where you load up your tool box. That's where you hone your skills. So, for instance, [when I'm designing something, and] I've decided I want the thing to be dramatic, emotional, and hard-hitting . . . where do you go from there?

Well, where you go is to your reserves, your tool box. I've been looking at things, posters, jewelry, buildings, and so on for ten years and cataloging all this stuff. I've been seeing an album cover and saying, "Whoa, that's gorgeous!" And then—the important part—saying, "Why did I have that reaction? Why did I think that was so gorgeous? What is it about that? Is it the colors? Is it the form and the composition?" And you store that away.

Similarly, you might say, "This restaurant menu looks crappy." Most people would stop there. But the designer says, "Wait a minute. Why did I have that reaction? Why is this menu not delivering the way they intended it to?" And so you have this mental storehouse chock full of literally thousands of data points, of emotional reactions. So you have these tools that you can bring to bear when you decide you want this poster, say, an anti-war poster, to have these effects. Then you can take the next important step and say, "What are the ingredients that are likely to create those effects? Are they going to be contrasting colors, diagonal lines, or harsh interfaces bumping up against one another?" [Ideas] begin to present themselves from this storehouse.

It's about finding out what I like, but also finding out why I like it, examining the components. It's really about being a more active, aggressive analyst.

*Tim McCreight, metalworker*

---

When I was studying at Les Gobelins in Paris, every Friday we would look at the history of tapestry in France and the characteristics of each period and how tapestry developed and changed. It had an important influence on my development. Then I worked for a while at a gallery that dealt in ancient textiles doing conservation. Handling these works, in particular Andean tapestries, allowed me to develop the strong love of pattern and color so characteristic of my work.

I believe the history (of a craft), initially, is important in how we develop the making of our contemporary work. It gives us a starting point. Contemporary work grows out of historical work.

Every person has a history, you have a history, I have a history and we are all part of a cultural history. These all influence our creative process.

*Susan Martin Maffei, tapestry weaver*

Susan Martin Maffei. *Traffic*, 2001. Tapestry with cotton warp and wool, silk, and linen weft. 48" × 80". *Photographer: Susan Martin Maffei.*

The important thing to remember about visual design is that it is a skill, not a talent. Even if you don't consider yourself artistic, you can create pieces with strong visual design—you just have to study, and understand, the principles behind it. Artistry is learned, not inborn.

Design is a visual language. You wouldn't expect to be able to write without learning about the language. You don't have to learn everything about the language to be able to make use of it, but if you have no confidence in your use of it, you're not going to be able to.

*Tommye Scanlin, tapestry weaver*

# TECHNICAL DESIGN SKILLS

Technical design is the art of translating your design into a plan for construction. To plan your piece, you need to consider the practical aspects and work out the construction steps, as covered in chapter 7, "Practical Considerations." Creating a technical design for a project requires an understanding of how your medium behaves: what you can and can't do with it, and how to make things that will hold up to their intended use. Creating technical blueprints also means learning how to plan construction. The more complex and unusual the piece, the better your skills need to be.

Technical design skills can be tricky to learn. There are two basic approaches. The first is to start simple—adapt existing designs, or build easy, uncomplicated pieces. Starting simple allows you to figure out what is and isn't possible in the medium, and how to build the things that are possible. As you develop more skill in creating your own designs, you can tackle more ambitious projects.

The second approach is to just dive in. When you run into the inevitable snags, ask for help from more experienced people. You can find yourself a mentor, ask around your craft guild (if you have one), or inquire on a mailing list or online group dedicated to your craft.

# EXERCISE 9: DESIGN ANALYSIS

Look for a piece that you admire, preferably one that lies just outside your current abilities. Examine it closely, and try to figure out how it was built. While the exact details will vary depending on your craft, here are some questions that might prove helpful:

1. What is the structure of the piece? What parts does it have?
2. If the object is made of different parts joined together, how were the parts connected? In what order were they joined to construct the piece?
3. What techniques were used in the piece's construction?
4. What finishing techniques were applied to "polish" the work during the final stages of construction?
5. What skills would you need to acquire to make this piece?

Once you have completed your analysis, write brief instructions for constructing the piece. Imagine a reader with similar skills to yours. What would he or she want to know? What design sketches would the reader want to see in order to understand how to make a similar piece?

If you have difficulty with this exercise, start with a piece that already has published instructions (a project from a book or magazine, perhaps). Cover up the instructions and do the exercise based on the photographs of the finished product. Then check your answers against the published instructions.

---

# EXERCISE 10: ADAPTING A DESIGN

Take an existing design, one for which you have instructions or that you already know how to make, and think of ways to alter it. Don't just alter the visual design—change the functional design or the construction as well, so that it poses a technical challenge. If you need ideas on how to change the piece, chapter 9, "Evaluating Your Work-in-Progress," provides some guidance for finding things to adapt.

Lay out your proposed changes, either with a drawing or a verbal description, and do the "Design Analysis" exercise above to build a roadmap for your changes.

You need not follow your design analysis precisely when making the altered piece, of course. In fact, if you are following the Creative Cycle, you shouldn't. Instead, you should continue making changes as you go. But learning to think through a design completely will help develop your skills in technical design.

---

# CONSTRUCTION SKILLS

Finally, construction skills are the manual skills needed to fashion a piece. They are relatively easy to learn, at least at the basic level, because most classes, tutorials, and how-to books focus on construction skills.

You do not need to spend a lot of money to get information about construction techniques. For most techniques, a simple Web search is all you need to find a wealth of information. Books and magazines are relatively inexpensive, and many free instructional videos are available on YouTube. Online tutorials can be just as useful as books—often more so, since online tutorials typically cover individual techniques in much more detail, with more photos, than a book can.

Another excellent option for developing your construction skills is to take a class in person. While classes are undoubtedly more expensive than books and videos, they are also interactive. You can ask questions, get corrections, and learn from your fellow students' mistakes and triumphs. You can also ask your instructor for suggestions for further study, rather than having to work out a plan yourself.

Finally, practice. Don't just hop from one technique to the next—find one you like and then explore it. Make lots of samples in order to discover what is possible using the method you've chosen, and to develop your skills in applying it. Don't worry about creating a polished work. Your intent is to learn.

I think that technical skills are the sort of thing that need to be refined through practice. If [taking courses] is an option, it's always worth it.

When that isn't an option, then using the wealth of information that is available on YouTube and in books is really important because there are right ways to do things and wrong ways to do things. Not only from a safety standpoint, which concerns me as an instructor, but also from the standpoint of creating things that last—if your intention is for them to last, of course.

But nothing beats good old solid practice for perfecting a technique or a skill.

*Jane Dunnewold, surface design artist*

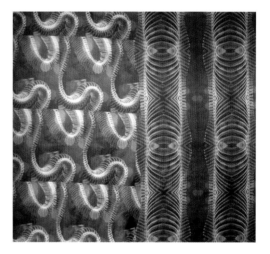

Jane Dunnewold. *Bone Dance*, 2014. Digitally printed fabric, assembled and backed, machine quilted. 70" × 70". *Photographer: Jane Dunnewold.* The design is made from photos of vertebrae taken at the Smithsonian National History Museum.

# EXERCISE 11: EXPLORING A TECHNIQUE

Choose a technique that interests you, and at which you are relatively unskilled. Find basic instructions for using the method you've chosen. Follow the instructions and repeat the tutorial project in small variations, perhaps changing the color or the pattern, until you feel you have a basic understanding of the skill.

Next, explore what you can do with the technique. You can do this systematically—for example, dyeing yarns to produce a complete color palette—or you can simply play around. Keep notes on what you are doing, so you can remember it later. If possible, keep some of the more interesting samples. If you feel like it, do a few small projects using this technique.

Now, think of other ways to apply the technique. Can you combine it with methods you already know? Pick one of your favorite skills and try to combine the two. Create more samples. Then come up with a simple project using both techniques. (Keep it simple, though—the intent is to practice and explore, not to spend a month building a large project.)

Finally, once you are comfortable with the technique, incorporate it into your major projects. Play several rounds of Design Poker (outlined in chapter 6, "Getting Started") using the technique as one of your idea cards. Build your projects from there.

---

# LEARN FROM OTHERS

Finding a mentor will help you develop all four skills much faster than going at it on your own. A mentor can answer your design and construction questions as you go, and will know your skills well enough to recommend techniques and projects that will be feasible. However, since you will likely be taking up your mentor's time on a regular basis, do make sure you repay your mentor somehow. This could be money (professional teachers will almost certainly charge a fee), barter, or a gift of some sort—something to show your appreciation for the time they're investing in you.

Don't be afraid to ask successful people for advice. More often than not, people will be happy to help out, and you can learn a lot that way.

My good friend, Ann Morhauser of Annieglass, when she first started, was great at introducing herself to people that she really admired and saying, "Hey, can I take you to lunch?" She would ask them about how it was [to work in the business], and how they started their business. She was so charming that, more often than not, they said, "Yeah, absolutely." So she gleaned ideas from these other people. They're not secrets—I mean, they're obvious things that people have figured out, but they seem like secrets to you until someone points you in the right direction.

So she was really great at that. And I would suggest that highly to anybody that's getting started, if you can do it in a very friendly and nice way. Most people are very willing to share, most people love to talk about themselves. If you ask them, "What do you attribute your success to?" more often than not they're going to tell you. [Talking to successful artisans] really was a great thing for her, and me as well. I was never bashful about learning from someone else.

*Guy Corrie, glassblower*

---

# DO THE WORK

However you choose to develop your skills, you will need to practice. You don't need to do it all at once; in fact, it's better to focus on one skill at a time, as the more unfamiliar things you attempt, the less likely you are to succeed at any of them. So if you are trying a new visual design concept in a piece, simplify your lesson by sticking to the familiar in its other design aspects and in its construction.

Your progress may seem slow at first. But by doing the work, constantly practicing and improving, you'll gradually improve in all four areas.

You learn by doing it. I could tell you all week how to ride a bicycle, but until you get on the bicycle you really don't have a clue.

You grow your talent by working. I'm a workaholic. I work really hard, and I feel like that's what allows me to grow my talent. The more you do, and the more different things you do, the bigger your vocabulary.

*Paul Marioni, glass artist*

---

Paul Marioni.

Be prepared for the long journey. One of the benefits of youth, and one of the dangers, is to think that things move too fast. I've had students who get upset and say, "Come on! I've been doing this for six months, and I'm not famous yet!" Well, maybe you need to develop a bigger view. Maybe it's going to take a while.

Within the twentieth century, probably the last quarter of the twentieth century, [you see] this rise to stardom, to instant fame. Who's out there on the magazine covers, making money and being interviewed on the radio? It's a twenty-two-year-old musician, a twenty-six-year-old athlete, and so on. And there's nothing wrong with that. But I think it's also worth reminding people that you don't have to hit the cover of a magazine before you're twenty-five.

So that's one thing I would say to someone who's just starting out. Be prepared for the long haul.

*Tim McCreight, metalworker*

Tim McCreight. *Untitled (Brooch)*, 2007. Fine silver. 2.75" × 2.75".
*Photographer: Robert Diamante.*

# TIME MANAGEMENT SKILLS

Often a piece comes with a deadline—an exhibit entry deadline, an upcoming show, or a promised commission for a client. If you're concerned with missing a delivery date, time management skills become critical. Here are some project management techniques that may be useful.

Start by estimating the effort using the techniques from chapter 7, "Practical Considerations." Don't forget to add an extra 30% to 100% to your estimates.

Once you've estimated the effort for each step, give yourself interim milestones to make sure you're on track, time-wise. Place your milestones far enough apart that you aren't constantly fiddling with them, but close enough together that you'll get advance warning should something be taking longer than expected. You can place milestones at the end of each step, or else have weekly goals based on your overall schedule. Or choose another scheme; the idea is to have a way to check in regularly to make sure that you're on track to complete in time.

If you start missing milestone dates, especially major ones, you'll likely want to rethink your design. Try to simplify and streamline construction to bring yourself back on track. Do you really need time-consuming, hand-carved scrollwork on your piece? If you do feel you need it, can you find someone else to help make it? These choices can be difficult, but they are essential if you want to avoid last-minute panic, late nights, and missed deadlines.

Another strategy for minimizing schedule risk is to do the most essential parts first. That way, if you run out of time, the important components of the design will be there, even if it isn't perfect. For example, if you build the legs and seat of a chair first, if you run out of time, you can drastically simplify the design and still be okay. But if you've spent your time hand-carving details into the back of the chair, and you run out of time, there's no way to recover.

Another way to reduce uncertainty in your overall schedule is by doing the most ambiguous parts first. Those might be steps where you don't know how long it will take, or steps where you're likely to make mistakes. Getting the dangerous parts out of the way early will render the rest of your schedule more predictable.

# EXERCISE 12: MAKING A CONSTRUCTION TIMELINE

1. Lay out what needs to be built. Keep it high-level. For example, if you are building a chair, you might need to build the legs, seat, and back, and then assemble the parts.

2. For each major part, estimate how long it will take you to create:

   a. The rough shape of the part

   b. Finer details

   c. Finishing touches

3. Identify the parts you consider the most essential, the areas that are riskiest, and the ones where you are least certain how long they will take.

4. Put together a construction plan, building in the following order:

   a. The rough outline of the most essential parts (including assembly)

   b. Finer details, starting with the riskiest parts, then the ones with the most uncertain estimates. (Often these will be the same.)

   c. Finishing touches

5. Make a ballpark estimate for how long it will take you to build the rough outline, then the detail work, and the finishing touches. Remember that you may change your design at any time during construction, so don't spend too much time on producing a detailed estimate.

6. Based on your ballpark estimate, create an estimated date for finishing each major step. These are your big milestones.

7. As you reach each construction step, break the big milestones down into smaller ones. Make the milestones progressively smaller until you get to a comfortable spot. The intent is to break things up so you get quick feedback on whether you're on the right track—that may mean weekly or monthly goals. Don't go beyond one milestone every two to three days—it won't buy you additional schedule accuracy and could drive you crazy.

---

# FINE-TUNING YOUR PROCESS

In addition to improving your skills, you'll want to improve your process, making it more enjoyable and effective, with less wasted effort. You can find some references on the creative process in the Recommended Reading section of this book, which may provide inspiration for approaches to try. But the majority of process improvement simply comes from reflecting on your process after each project.

Do Exercise 7, "Improving your process." How can you do more of the things you enjoyed, and less of the things you didn't? Could you have avoided a mistake by making the piece differently? Pick one or two ideas to incorporate into your process in the next project. The changes may seem small, but over time, they'll make a big difference.

# 13

# FINDING YOUR VOICE

There is almost nothing that hasn't been done. Originality is only doing it in your own way.

*Paul Marioni, glass artist*

---

One challenge that many new artisans face is finding their creative voice—a style that is clearly and uniquely theirs. It's tempting to dabble in this and that, trying techniques and styles one after another, but this can lead to the artistic version of multiple personality disorder. As one student ruefully told surface design artist Jane Dunnewold, "I do so many different things, I could have my own group show!"

Does having "a voice" matter? It depends on your artistic goals. If you are making your work strictly for yourself or for casual sales, finding your artistic voice isn't necessary. But if you are trying to develop a career as an artist, particularly for high-end galleries, you will need to develop a distinctive style.

Fortunately, finding your voice is not a mystical process. As you work, you will naturally develop your own personal style, but there are some ways to speed up the process.

## UNDERSTAND WHAT YOU LIKE

First, understand your personal preferences. Go through your house and pull out things you like—personal items like clothing, jewelry, and furniture, or things in your inspiration book. What do they have in common? Do you see any of those themes reflected in your work?

It's funny. Something like 80% of the time, when I'm teaching, people start their projects and [the color of] a person's project is the color that they are wearing.

*Andrea Graham, felter*

---

Next, look at your existing work to find common elements. If something appears repeatedly, it probably is (or could become) a part of your voice. Is it something you'd like to develop further? If so, think of ways to incorporate it into your next few projects. Make it part of your artistic style.

If you look at some of the pieces [an artist] has made, say ten pieces, what do they look like? Are they all shiny metal? Has he or she used blue lapis in all the pieces? What about those ten pieces does he or she love? And that is usually the maker's artistic voice, even if he or she didn't realize it. Most people will like a shape, a color, or a texture, and that will show up in much of their work.

Once you discover your style and your voice, you can increase your creativity. You don't have to be limited. You can develop that voice, and take it off in different directions.

*Debora Mauser, metalworker*

---

Once you've looked at your finished pieces for design themes, look at your construction process. Are there techniques or materials you consistently enjoy and use? They may be part of your voice as well. Experiment with incorporating them into other aspects of your work.

I think that you can develop your voice by seeing what things fascinate you. Like when you're working, and you lose all track of time. You don't get hungry, and you don't notice that the day is going by. Then whatever you're doing is in the sweet spot. That is the feeling everyone's trying to get. And when you can climb into that quicker and quicker, that's a natural way to feel the direction of your voice.

So find a positive obsession. Make sure that whatever you want to make, there's a piece of it that makes you want to go back and research or look at something. Looking through any kind of history, there's going to be something, somewhere that will just blow your mind. Whether it's hair jewelry, or indigo dyeing, or the like, find the thing that you think is coolest. Research it and learn it.

I talked to this young woman the other day who is a jeweler. What can you possibly do that's new? Well, she has latched onto this material, jet. It's a kind of stone, and she is obsessed with it. Her enthusiasm, telling me about what she's doing and how she's doing it, was so beautiful.

Find something that you can really throw yourself into. Your voice will come out of that.

*Ellen Wieske, metalworker*

Ellen Wieske. *50 Valentine's Pins to Give Away*, 2013. Tin. 2" × 1". *Photographer: Ellen Wieske.*

Once you understand your preferences, think about how to synthesize your favorite techniques, materials, and design elements into something that is stylistically yours. Don't just imitate your favorite teacher—take the technique, or the design style, and incorporate it into your own style and repertoire.

There's an expectation that if you are going to go out into the world and show your work, there should be a departure [from the techniques and style of your teacher]. I think there are some people who don't know that going out and doing work that's derivative of another artist is not ok. It's great for you to do this in a class, but now [as a teacher] I want you to take those techniques and make them your own.

*Andrea Graham, felter*

# EXERCISE 13: UNDERSTANDING WHAT MATTERS TO YOU

Find ten or so of your favorite belongings. They need not be handmade or of exceptional quality. Look at them. Why do you like them? Don't limit yourself to things like color, materials, and other concrete things. Think also about immaterial things like style, symbolism, personal meaning. What makes it important to you? Perhaps it was made by a favorite uncle. Or maybe it's a historical relic. Or you just like Art Deco style, or the color green. Write down what makes each attractive to you.

Now, look at your list for common themes. Are there characteristics that appear in multiple objects? Or is there a distinctive feature in one object that you feel strongly about? Mark these as possible elements of your artistic voice.

By studying closely the things that you love, you will get a better understanding of what matters to you—not just your favorite styles, colors, and materials, but also your personal values. These can all become part of your artistic voice.

# EXERCISE 14: UNDERSTANDING WHAT BRINGS YOU JOY

Take out five to ten of your favorite finished pieces—works that you enjoyed making, or pieces you love. Think about what makes them your favorites. As with the previous exercise, think about the piece's characteristics, and consider intangibles like style and meaning as well as more concrete characteristics such as size, materials, and aesthetics.

More importantly, think about the process of making it. What did you enjoy about making each piece? Did you like working with a particular material, or are you fascinated by a technique? Perhaps you found it meditative, or exhilarating. Or maybe working on it reminded you of a favorite person or a happy event. Did you learn something interesting while making it? Write down why making these pieces brought you joy.

Working through this exercise will help you better understand both what you are proud of in your work, and what you most enjoy. Emphasizing enjoyment is important: Techniques may come and go, materials may lose their attraction, but the things you enjoy are what will keep you working in your craft.

# EXERCISE 15: TRANSLATING YOUR PREFERENCES INTO NEW WORK

Now that you understand your personal preferences, both in what you find attractive and what you enjoy making, let's put your new knowledge into action.

Write your preferences on index cards, and separate them into two categories: what you love about an object (color, materials, style, etc.) and what you love about the process of working in your craft. Draw three cards from each deck, and play Design Poker (described in chapter 6, "Getting Started"), brainstorming designs drawn from those six cards. Do any of those designs particularly appeal to you? What makes them the most appealing?

The intent of this exercise isn't to create designs for your next project (though it would be great if it does), but to give you some insight into what appeals to you and how to translate those preferences into new work. These insights, gathered over time, will help you develop your distinctive style.

## DON'T BE SWAYED BY OTHERS

Try not to pay too much attention to others' opinions. Especially as a new artist, it's tempting to focus on what will please others: friends, fellow guild members, show judges, teachers, etc. While others' feedback is valuable, take it as suggestions—you're still the one in charge. And while winning prizes is fun, paying too much attention to others can drown out your own creative voice. So take care to separate your own feelings about your work from the feelings of others. Listen to your own voice—it's far more important than the world's.

Some people worry way too much at the beginning about what other people think about what they're doing. I think we have to try not to care so much about what other people think, so we can discover what we ourselves care about and think.

*Jane Dunnewold, surface design artist*

Paul Marioni. *DALI*, 1972.
Stained glass with
removable eye, door in
throat. Glass, lead, Fresnel
lenses. 27" × 25" × 0.5".
*Photographer:*
*Jack Fulton.*

I think the only person that can critique my work is me. I don't give a shit what the critics think. In fact I'll often laugh. Bill Morris [the glass artist] once said that he wished the critics would mind their own business. It's like, they've got their own agenda. They have their own way of seeing things.

To me it's not important if you are satisfied with what you made. Because you have to live with it. Did it do what you wanted it to do? If you had to make it over, would you change anything? Aspects like that are what's important.

*Paul Marioni, glass artist*

You may find that developing your own style means inventing new techniques, or breaking the unspoken rules of your medium. Don't be afraid to innovate. Your objective is to develop a distinctive voice, and developing new techniques and approaches is a great way to accomplish that. Not everyone will accept your innovations, and that's okay. Artistically speaking, the only opinion that really matters about your work is yours.

Sometimes you want to do something, and the traditional way to do it just doesn't work. So you have to improvise.

It may be that the only way you can think of to make it work is to do something that is not acceptable to the field that you're in. But it's the only way you can think of to make it work. So you do it. Pretty soon other people might follow. What was unacceptable, at one time, can become a new genre.

I've done that in several aspects in the quilting world over the years. You get exasperated because something doesn't work because you're trying to do it in the traditional format, and your ideas are going beyond the traditional format. So you have to figure it out, and it may be totally against all the rules, but that's okay.

In the '70s I was trying to do some landscapes of mountains and water, and in those days appliqué was the only way that you worked with representational work. Trees were always triangles or round, bushes were always circles. There was a certain primitive way of working. I just couldn't get any sophistication out of working in that way and I was very frustrated.

I couldn't get the color gradations that I wanted. Sunrises and sunsets, the way the clouds formed—I just couldn't get that working in the accepted manner. Finally I got exasperated. I decided to cut out strips of fabric and make the pieces form as I was cutting them up and putting them together.

I started doing that, and it became its own genre. Nobody had ever seen it before. It's not something that I tried to invent—I did it out of a desire to do something that was in my soul, and my frustration. I couldn't get it to work the way that everybody else was doing it.

When my first quilt went to a show, there were two reactions to my work. One was those who thought it was amazing and loved it and wanted to do it. And then there were the people who reacted, "Who does she think she is? This is terrible, she's not doing this the right way."

But it became its own genre.

*Joen Wolfrom, quilter*

Joen Wolfrom. *Catch a Falling Star on a Hot August Night*, 1990. Quilt sewn from cotton fabrics, 60" × 75". *Photographer: Ken Wagner.*

Rachel Carren. *Sporting Life*, 2014. Polymer, paper, silk, polyester ribbon. 22" × 17" × 12". *Photographer: Greg Staley.*

I got really fascinated, maybe because I'm a middle-aged woman, with how the younger women were dressing. I started to think seriously about the meaning of culture and clothing and how they interact and interface.

I began to do a lot of reading on the subject, and decided I wanted to figure out a way to make clothing out of polymer.

A few others had already explored the idea, but I wanted to do something too. My initial idea

Rachel Carren. Detail, *Sporting Life*, 2014. Polymer, paper, silk, polyester ribbon. 22" × 17" × 12". *Photographer: Greg Staley.*

was related to my disc collar necklaces which have internal threading that allows them to drape. I was thinking I could create some system with the discs to make a sheet of drapeable surface. However, internal threading wouldn't work with the greatly expanded size of a garment such as a vest.

I quickly abandoned the idea. Then I thought, well, you know, clothing is made out of cloth. Maybe I can figure out how to weave polymer. So I ended up figuring out how to weave polymer into cloth.

It was an incredibly complicated process. It took me the better part of two years from having the idea, to figure out how to do it. I would solve one problem and move on. It was like inching forward, and every step was a new problem that had to be resolved.

I finally was able to do it and the result was part of an exhibition.

*Rachel Carren, polymer artist*

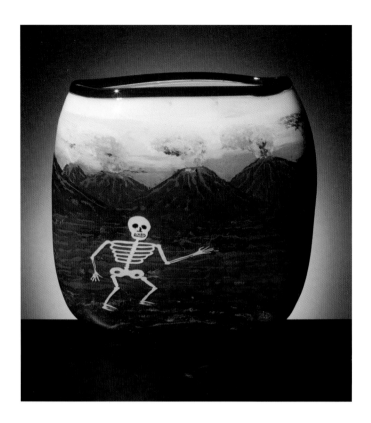

Paul Marioni, *OOOOHAHA*, 2005. Painted and blown glass. 10" × 11" × 3". *Photographer: Russell Johnson.*

My generation started the studio glass movement. I'm considered one of the pioneers, one of a handful of people who started it.

Glass has a five-thousand-year history. It was a very carefully guarded secret in industry. Artists never really had a chance. Artists sometimes designed for glass, but they never made the glass. And then we came along. My generation, we basically stole the fire.

Initially industry wouldn't help us. It was a closed door. We couldn't get in. We had to figure out how to melt glass, how to make color, how to blow glass, how to cast glass. We had to figure all that out ourselves. But we didn't have any preconceived notions about what should be done. We just thought about what could be done, and we weren't in industry so we didn't have to make a profit.

In fact I sometimes joke, "What were we thinking??" When we got started there were no schools, no materials, no collectors, no galleries, no museum shows, no books. There was nothing. What were we thinking? I joke that obviously we *weren't* thinking!

We just saw the potential.

*Paul Marioni, glass artist*

The final aspect of finding your creative voice is integrity. Do your best work, and assess it honestly. Your work doesn't have to be technically perfect, but it needs to reflect the best that you can do. Without integrity, your voice will lack authority.

There's an old saying, I think from the Shaker tradition, which I never understood earlier: "Do your work as if you would live forever and as if you would die tomorrow."

I've reached an understanding of that because of the circumstances of where I live. I live in an old mill on a flood plain. In order to have a water-powered mill, you have to build on the water.

Well, when the hurricanes come and the water rises, everything goes under water. So there's always this question, when I'm doing work here, on the building: "Why should I do top-quality work if I know it's going to go under water at some point?"

It could be this year, it could be in six years, but sooner rather than later, it's going to be under water and likely be ruined. And so why do quality work?

I struggled with this for a long time and then it slowly emerged in my brain that everything gets washed away. That's the reality of things. But it's not a reason not to do your very best. Even though it's going to go away, even though you know it isn't going to last forever.

If you don't, if you don't do the best you can, you're missing something. You're always living at a shoddy level. So, for its own sake, do everything as well as it can be done.

*Roy Underhill, woodworker*

Roy Underhill at work.

# SELLING YOUR WORK

If you are planning to sell professionally, you'll have to choose a venue. There are two major venues for making a living from craft. The first is high-end galleries, collectors, and museums, where each piece is expected to be a unique artistic expression. The second is craft shows and wholesale markets, where you will typically develop a product line that can be developed in variations and reliably repeated.

These two venues are not mutually exclusive. Juried craft shows that focus on quality and expression will attract collectors. But if you plan to make a living from craft, you will be best served by focusing on one of these two venues, as the route to success can be quite different between the two.

## SELLING UNIQUE WORKS OF ART

Making a living by creating and selling unique works of craftsmanship is not easy. In order to reach your customers, you'll need access to high-end galleries and other similar artistic venues. This, in turn, means you need to develop a reputation and a distinctive style—one that will enable collectors to identify your work. You'll also need to network a lot—talking to gallery owners and museum curators about showing and selling your work.

Developing your reputation means showing your work—at local shows initially, as you hone your skills and your voice, and eventually graduating to regional, national, and international venues. Juried shows typically have more prestige, so focus on those as you build your reputation. Pay close attention to the goals and entry guidelines for the show to avoid wasting your time on shows that don't suit your style.

Because most shows are juried from photos, good photography is essential. Learn how to photograph your pieces, or hire a professional photographer. People deciding whether to select or represent your work will be doing so based on the photos you send—so if you don't photograph the work well, even a great piece is likely to be rejected.

The way these [high-end craft] shows were juried, and I'm sure many are still the same, the juror looked at five images from each artist simultaneously, all projected at once. So the continuity of the background, and the design concepts, and the look and feel of the work, were very important to show that there was a cohesive sort of design plan there.

Of course, execution and quality of the work [mattered too]. But when I juried, I would see people I knew. I knew the quality of their work was great, but the presentation was so poor in these slide presentations that you couldn't give them as high marks as other people. It was frustrating. Somebody had a beautiful cut-glass window, and it was shown with a hand holding it up outside next to the '55 Mercury. It was just horrible. It completely took away from the work.

So absolutely, the best photography collateral materials you can have, and the most cohesive look, is the way to approach getting into one of these shows.

*Guy Corrie, glassblower*

## EXERCISE 16: SELECTING SHOWS TO ENTER

Find a list of shows that feature works in your chosen medium. You can find these shows through the *Craft Marketplace* series of books, event listings in magazines, a craft association website, or Web searches. Or ask established artists what shows they recommend.

Research each venue. First, read through the entry guidelines (often called a *prospectus*). Does your work fit the guidelines? If there is a geographical restriction, note that; if there is a theme to the show, make sure your work fits the theme.

Next, look at works that have been juried into the show in previous years. Is your work of equal or greater quality? If so, you have a much better chance of getting into the show.

What is the reputation of the show? Is it a small, local exhibit, or a well-known national competition? When it comes to your artistic resume, prestigious shows will carry more weight than more modest exhibits, but it is easier to gain entry (and win awards) in a cozier venue.

Consider entry fees, and the cost of shipping your work to and from the exhibit. Many shows require you to insure your work during shipping, which can be expensive for valuable pieces.

Also check whether your venue insures the pieces while they are on exhibit. Major shows almost certainly will, but smaller exhibits may not. Depending on the value of your work, that may or may not matter to you.

Once you've gathered sufficient information, you'll be in a good position to evaluate whether entering the show is worthwhile.

You will also want to develop your personal style. While you don't want to duplicate items exactly, developing a distinctive look is essential to succeeding in the artists' market. While your voice will develop naturally over time, you can speed the process by thinking deliberately about your preferences, as described in chapter 13, "Finding Your Voice."

You have to know your intention. If you're just looking to make stuff to have a social afternoon, to do something creative and visit with your friends, you don't have to have a style. But if your intention is to participate at the highest level of craft and to really make a statement, then you do have to have a voice and you do have to have a style.

As soon as you start to ask people for money for your work, then your intentions are a little bit bigger and a little bit different and it starts to matter. If you have any dreams about someday having your work be seen at a place like the Museum of Art and Design or the Metropolitan Museum of Art, then you really do need to have a very firm sense of who and what you're about. You're not going to get there without it.

*Rachel Carren, polymer artist*

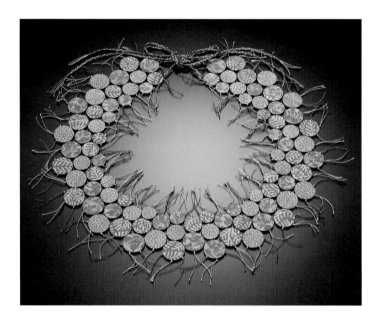

Rachel Carren. *William Morris Reversible Disk Collar*, 2010. Polymer, acrylic pigment, silk, wire, glass beads. 14" × 14" × 0.125". *Photographer: Hap Sakwa.*

Paul Marioni. *ALL IT TAKES*, 1974. Broken window glass. 22" × 18" × 0.125". From the series *Light Poems*. Photographer: Jack Fulton.

You need to be bold. Opportunity doesn't knock on anybody's door like it did when I was young. Opportunity is now fleeing with thousands of people in hot pursuit. So you need to be bold. You need to stand out above the crowd. All the time I hear people say, "Well, a lot of glass is mediocre." And I say, "Well a lot of painting is mediocre, a lot of ceramics is mediocre. A lot of doctors and plumbers are mediocre." You've got to stand out. You've got to be bold. You've got to get out there and do something that will make people notice.

And I've been really lucky because I have been really bold. I've gotten opportunities to do a lot of different things.

So I tell people, just be bold. Stand out. Don't be timid about showing people who you are and what you can do.

*Paul Marioni, glass artist*

Once you begin to develop a reputation, think about venues for publication. What books and magazines are written about your craft? What kinds of artists do they write about? Ideally, you want to be published in forums that target your chosen market. For most artists, this means that books and magazines that publish articles about unique craftworks and master artisans, such as *American Craft,* are better venues than "how-to" magazines targeted at hobbyists. There is overlap, of course—hobbyist magazines often profile artists—but writing how-to articles will generally not further your artistic reputation.

Galleries are another critical venue for showing and selling your work. Do a Web search for galleries that represent artists in your craft. Research each gallery by looking at the artists they currently represent. Are their style and skill level similar to yours? Then consider approaching the gallery about representing your work. (And note down the galleries that are representing artists whose skill and reputation exceed yours: you'll want to approach them in a few years, as you grow.)

Consider a group exhibit, too—getting a group of artists together to create an exhibit, then looking for a venue. Particularly when you are just starting out, this can be an effective way of getting your work shown.

Our first exhibit that we put together, we met for months and months and months, the five of us, and we ended up having our first venue at the San Francisco Art Institute, which is across the street from City Hall. I actually got two commissions out of that show, and that's the show that traveled to Georgia, the one my dealer saw.

My son is an artist and he has done the same thing. He'll get five or six or ten artists together. They will put together a show and then go to a gallery and say "We've got this show, do you have an open space? I'm coming in with ten artists, and we have these media." And that's worked very well for him.

So that's one way of getting your work into an exhibit. And then we do a small exhibit catalog. It was very reasonable to do a small catalog, with only five of us. And then you've got that catalog forever.

*Yvonne Porcella, quilter*

Another important sales tool is a professional-looking website. While you may not sell many pieces directly, a good website is a powerful sales tool—a place where people can see your portfolio, your artist's statement, and your resume. Include your website address in your e-mail's signature line, so the curious can find out more about you.

One of the most important things is to have a website that looks great, with really good photography. Contact the gallery and say, "Can you advise me as to your submission policy, or tell me how you consider artists?" If you've got a really great looking website, and you put it in your signature line, you know they are going to click on it.

*Andrea Graham, felter*

---

Finally, you'll need to network. Get out and talk to people: gallery owners, museum curators, and so on. Ask those people to introduce you to other people. Go to opening receptions and shows. Keep everyone's contact information organized. As your reputation and your network grow, a good contact list will be essential to growing your market.

Because developing a reputation typically takes years, don't give up your day job, at least not immediately.

Being an artist and working for yourself, you have to promote yourself, so I travel a lot. When I go places I generally tend to go see directors of museums, talk to them about what's going on, what I'm doing, what my friends are doing, and what opportunities there are in the future. That way, people know who I am and what I am capable of doing.

*Paul Marioni, glass artist*

People say, "Oh my gosh! You're being invited all over the world, you're in this magazine and that magazine." Well, none of this happened without my working really, really hard. Here's how it evolved for me:

I would say that the first five years was really just exploring the craft. Maybe I taught a very low-level beginner class. As my skills moved up a level, I would teach the next lower levels, like climbing up stairs.

[Since then] it's been a slow evolution. I started by entering local juried shows, and after I got recognition provincially, I went national. I was always stretching myself and setting goals for the next level, saying to myself, "Okay, what is the next big thing?" In the next few years my goal might be to be on the cover of a particular magazine. And so I'd put steps into place. I'd send the editor a letter. They might say "No, we're not interested." But I've started. And maybe once they see my work several times, four years later, it'll happen.

So it's a constant thing, like a hamster wheel.

*Andrea Graham, felter*

---

# CREATING AND SELLING A PRODUCT LINE

If you're planning to create and sell a product line, rather than one-of-a-kind artistic works, you'll want to start by choosing a venue in which to sell. You can sell directly to the public, usually through craft shows, a website, or an online marketplace. Or you can sell wholesale, typically to a gallery or an online or department store that will then resell your work.

Which is most effective? It depends on what you are selling, how much you intend to sell, and your own skills and inclinations. If you are only planning to sell a few items, a small gallery may be perfect for your needs. If you love chatting with your customers, and are producing in large enough volume to fill a booth, a craft show will allow you to meet the public. And if you want to grow into a production studio, you will eventually want to sell wholesale to larger distributors.

In general, you can sell larger volumes of work through wholesale, but at much lower prices. Because the reseller also needs to make a profit, expect to get only about 50% of your retail price when selling through a gallery, department store, or other reseller.

At the beginning, you'll want to start small, either supplying a few shops, selling through a low-volume website, or doing one or two low-key craft shows. That will give you a sense for the business—what type of people will buy your work, which venues you enjoy selling through, and whether you can make a profit selling what you're selling. The "sweet spot" for sales is the intersection between what you want to make and what the customer is willing to buy at a price that makes both of you happy.

Don't get too discouraged if your initial sales are slow. It takes time to build a customer base. If you plan to work full-time making craftwork, it will take years—even a decade—to get enough experience, reputation, and customer following to make your entire living from it.

As you get a feel for the market and the business and want to expand your sales, you'll want to think carefully about your target market. Consider the *Who* and *Why* from chapter 4, "Functional Design." Think about your sales venues, and choose venues where your market is likely to find you. And consider tailoring your work so it appeals to customers at your chosen venue and in your target market. Don't lose sight of your own vision and passion, but try to find as much room as you can in the intersection between what you want to make and what people are willing to buy.

You know, I never design completely for the public. You have to design for what's pleasing to you, and then you find out where your sensibilities lie with the buying public. If they have some alignment, then you're going to be successful [as a production artisan]. If not, then you're going to be more of a one-of-a-kind artist, and you're looking for that sort of niche customer and/or collector.

So you develop a sensibility. You can see what's in the market, and you can see where you fit. I think a big problem for most people is that they're not really sure what market they need to be in.

*Guy Corrie, glassblower*

Guy Corrie. *Morph*, 2004. *Photographer: Paul Berg.*

In a painting world, a photography world, sometimes that's more about what you want to present at an exhibit. It's more about your own content. But in retail for clothing and retail for hats or jewelry, you need to be in touch with what people actually are saying about your work and what needs you might be able to fill.

Carolyn, the owner of Fino Fino, a store I sold to for nineteen years, tells this story to new designers who approach her regarding hat sales. She says, "Wayne was the only designer who ever called me and said 'What do you need?'"

What this told her was that it's less about what I'm generating, and more about what I can create and will work for you. That impressed her so much . . . Because often designers work in isolation. They create a line, they take it to a rep, the rep tries to sell it, and the store buyers decide what to purchase for their customers. I'm thinking, "Why don't we go the other way? I can do anything. What do you need?"

*Wayne Wichern, milliner*

Wayne Wichern. *Erte Headpiece*, 2014. Velour felt, iridescent glass beads. 8" × 14" × 8". *Photographer: Wayne Wichern.*

Wayne Wichern. *Rose Garden*, 2011. Red felt, black rayon. 11" × 6" × 10". *Photographer: Wayne Wichern.*

Wayne Wichern. *Brocade Swirl Brim*, 2012. Raspberry parisisal straw, silk/rayon brocade. 16" × 8" × 10". *Photographer: Wayne Wichern.*

Wayne Wichern. *Rose Garden*, 2015. Navy parisisal straw, dupioni silk, chenille dot veiling, silk roses. 18" × 8" × 14". *Photographer: Wayne Wichern.*

Wayne Wichern. *Grande Rose*, 2012. Velour felt, silk velvet. 12" × 7" × 10". *Photographer: Wayne Wichern.*

As you think through your market, you will probably find some tension between what you want to make and what people are willing to buy. At one end of the spectrum, you can simply make what you feel like making, and hope people buy it. Making what you want gives you considerable artistic freedom, but at the cost of fewer sales. At the other end of the spectrum, you can focus entirely on what will sell—which will bring in higher sales, but may not allow you to express the passion that originally attracted you to the craft.

In my twenties and thirties, I wanted to make sure we could put food on the table. That was a driving factor in trying to produce pieces that were somewhat commercial, so that there was a market for them and I could sell.

Now forty years, fifty years later, I don't really have those financial burdens. So it's a lot easier to make things that I just want to experiment with. I don't know if that makes me more creative or not, but I don't have that burden, that responsibility of bringing in an income. That's been quite nice in that I can "play" with clay in the flames of my wood-fired kiln.

I live a lifestyle that doesn't require that much money. So for the last ten years, I probably live on $10,000 to 12,000 a year, so I can make things that I want to make.

*Hiroshi Ogawa, ceramicist*

Hiroshi Ogawa. *Ichirin Zashi #7*. Wood-fired clay. 7" × 14" × 7". *Courtesy of Eutectic Gallery*.

What's funny is, for me I never found [artistic freedom vs. market requirements] to be a conflict. I know a lot of people think that it's a conflict, but I never saw it that way. I spent twenty years working as a designer, where you will always need the client's final approval on anything you work on. So for me, being free of that constraint feels like a complete state of creative freedom.

There's a side of a pottery business which is, "Will it sell? How much will it sell for?" But . . . from the perspective of having been a designer for twenty years, everything about the pottery business feels like complete freedom.

*Mea Rhee, potter*

Mea Rhee's *Good Elephant* show booth. *Courtesy of Mea Rhee. Photographer: Mea Rhee.*

You'll also want to think about marketing. If you are selling retail, your single most valuable marketing asset is your mailing list—people who have seen your work and who want to know what you are up to and where you will be selling. So if you are selling at shows, put a signup sheet for your mailing list somewhere in your booth. If you are selling online, include a mailing list sign-up box prominently on your website. Send out notices when you are doing a show or sale, or introducing a new product line. This will reach an already-loyal following.

To succeed, you'll also need to find new customers. Where you find those customers depends on what you are selling. If you are selling things that people prefer to see and touch before buying, like clothing, then craft shows, galleries, or other venues where customers can physically interact with your work are probably the best option. But if you plan to sell primarily through a website, go find your customers online, through social media or Web advertising.

Once you've found your customers, think about pricing. Look at your competition, especially established artisans that are making a living from their work. How much are they charging for similar items? That will give you a sense for what the market will bear.

[I sell most of my work at shows, so] the largest aspect of my marketing is researching and finding the right shows to be in. Being in those shows is a marketing message in itself: "I made it into this nice, high quality show." Then, people that you meet there are your target market. So for me, that's the largest part of introducing myself to the people I need to meet.

I also write a blog, which I understand is very popular amongst potters. I don't know how many customers read that blog, but I know a lot of potters read it. So amongst potters, a lot of people know who I am, just because of my writing. Whenever I'm at a show, people walk up to me regularly and say how much they love my blog. They don't necessarily buy anything, but they know who I am because of my blog.

I do Facebook. I have a business page for Facebook, and I announce my shows, and I occasionally make other posts such as, "This is a new pot I'm working on," or, "I just wrote a new blog post. Go read it."

That's about it in terms of social media. Facebook doesn't necessarily generate attendance at shows. A lot of my Facebook followers are in faraway places, and they're not going to attend my shows. Sometimes I wonder if it's worth it.

My mailing list is hugely important. At every show, I have a pad in my display that says, "Sign up for my mailing list." Then people sign up for my mailing list through my website as well, but not as much. By far, the most people who are on my mailing list sign up for it at a show. They're people whom I've met in person. Every time I do a show, I do a blast email to that mailing list, which is now over 1,000 people, and that is a very, very important marketing tool. I think direct email marketing is so much more important than Facebook because those people, like I said, mostly have already seen my work in person and I've met them in person. And for people who attend art festivals in my region, it's way more targeted, and it's way more effective.

*Mea Rhee, potter*

Well, it's no secret. You go out there and sell it and nobody buys it at $85, and you drop it to $55 and it sells, the secret's revealed. You're just out of your price point for this particular look.

*Guy Corrie, glassblower*

---

I have a range of prices. I design and make hats at a low price point, a medium price point and a higher price point. Then I have a range of hats for the variety of people who come to me. It's become more important because my current studio is open to the public. People poke their heads in the door and say, "Oh, hats. What are your prices?" That's the first question out of their mouths.

When you're dealing with a wholesale market or a customized situation, those people have experience, they know you, and they know your quality and price range. If I set every hat in my studio at a minimum $250, and they go up to $500, I'm cutting off the interest from a lot of people who are going to be gasping at the thought of an expensive hat. I can't compete with the $59 hat you might find at T.J.Maxx, or even Whole Foods. I realized I needed to come up with something that was a little less breathtaking, so I have been sourcing supplies and designing a few hats to accommodate a lower price point.

I can do a sewn beret for about $45. So now I can say, "I make hats anywhere from $45 to $500." I count on that to break the ice on pricing, and not make it awkward for people or myself. I usually add "But I can always make a more expensive hat." It adds a bit of humor. It also tells them that this is a fluid situation, and that I'm an artist and I'm a practical business person. I'm trying to accommodate you, and we can work it out. What do you need?

*Wayne Wichern, milliner*

Wayne Wichern at work. *Photographer: Jason Wells.*

When I introduce a new pot to the public, it usually starts out pretty low priced—a prototype price. If it sells quickly, then I'll raise it a little for the next show. If it continues to sell well, then I'll keep raising the price in increments per show. As you can see, it takes a really long time. There are a lot of pots that I currently make where I raised the price two dollars too much at one point, and the sales just stopped. There was one show where just nobody bought it. I realized, "Okay, I know I went two dollars too far." So I just backed it down and it started selling again. That's when you know that you hit the sweet spot.

*Mea Rhee, potter*

Avoid pricing based on material costs or time plus materials. You will encounter many books and websites that suggest tripling material costs or paying yourself a "wage" in addition to material costs to arrive at pricing. However, your cost of production has nothing to do with what the customer will pay! So don't price based on your cost. Look around and see how much others are selling similar items for. Start your prices there initially, then tweak up and down depending on your sales.

## EXERCISE 17: SETTING PRICING

Decide on a venue in which to sell—craft shows, online marketplaces, or galleries. Explore the venue, and look at prices for items similar to yours. Compare the items to yours, assessing construction quality, design excellence, and the skill and experience needed to create each item. Find out whether the other vendors' products are selling at those prices. If you are researching craft shows, chat casually with the vendor: Are his or her pieces selling like hotcakes, or is business slow? In the first case, the price might be set too low; in the second, too high. (Of course, there are other reasons business might be slow, so take that as a hint, not as proof.)

Similarly, many online marketplaces will allow you to see how many of an item have been sold and at what prices. This will let you get a sense for the actual selling price of a piece.

Try to take your pricing cues from people who sell their craftwork for a living. Amateurs often underprice their products, either out of ignorance or because they don't need the money. Some will sell for less than the cost of materials! If you are selling professionally, you can't afford to do this. So when setting your prices, look to the pros, not the casual seller.

If you plan to sell for a living, pay close attention to profitability. Subtract the cost of materials, marketing costs, and overhead (studio rental, booth fees, etc.) from the final selling price for a piece. That is your profit. Divide by the number of hours invested in the piece—including the time spent marketing, etc.—and you have your hourly "salary" for making it. If you aren't making a living wage from the piece, you'll want to change how you make it, or else discontinue it.

In 2010, I was considering closing down my design studio and doing pottery full time. I was making a big decision, and I wanted more concrete knowledge. "Is this really smart, or is this really dumb?" So I spent a year figuring out how much I was actually making per hour working as a potter, and it gave me the peace of mind to know that if I were to give up my design job, I would be okay financially. For my design contracts, those were all based on hourly rates, so I knew I made roughly $100 an hour as a designer. At pottery, at the time, I thought, "I'm not even making minimum wage doing this." I had no idea. But I figured out my hourly wage working as a potter. In 2010, that worked out to be about $25 an hour doing wholesale, and about $32 an hour doing retail. Once I figured that out, over the course of a whole year, I gave myself permission to quit my design job, because I thought that was a reasonable amount to earn working as a potter. The whole motivation for spending a year doing it was to reassure myself that it was okay to quit my job.

I timed myself every day. I didn't really keep track of how much I was producing in the studio that day. I would take a wholesale order, and time myself for all the hours I took in order to complete that order. So that's throwing, trimming, handling, glazing, packing, studio cleanup. And then I took the dollar amount of the order, and I subtracted whatever expenses I knew I could quantify from that, like the cost of the shipping boxes, the cost of the clay, and then I divided that by the number of hours. Any time I had a chunk of income that I could analyze like that, I did. I did several wholesale orders in that way. I did four art festivals in that way. I took the final dollar amount that I made at the art festival, subtracted out the expenses that were involved in the art festival, and then calculated the number of hours I spent getting ready for the show, including making all of the pots and doing the show itself. Then I divided A by B to figure out how much I made per hour.

*Mea Rhee, potter*

## EXERCISE 18: HOW MUCH ARE YOU REALLY EARNING?

Use the worksheet on the next page to calculate your approximate earnings per hour when selling your work. If you don't know a particular expense, just put in your best guess. It's probably easiest to calculate this for a time period (such as a month or a year), but you can also do it for a specific show as long as you track your time to make the items sold at the show. Don't drive yourself crazy doing this: If a cost is minor and will be difficult to calculate, leave it out.

# EARNINGS WORKSHEET

## Income

| | |
|---|---|
| Income from selling your work | |
| **Total income:** | |

## Financial costs

| | |
|---|---|
| Studio rental | |
| Studio electricity and other utilities | |
| | |
| Materials | |
| Tools (purchase, repair, maintenance) | |
| | |
| Advertising costs for online and traditional marketing | |
| Show entry fees | |
| Travel costs for shows | |
| Cost of transporting your work to shows | |
| Booth expenses (electricity, furniture, loading/unloading) | |
| Shipping supplies and fees | |
| | |
| Shop fees (online or brick-and-mortar shops) | |
| Credit card processing fees | |
| Bank fees | |
| | |
| Accounting (if you hire others) | |
| Payroll, including taxes (if you have employees) | |
| Business license and other government fees | |
| Business insurance | |
| **Total costs:** | |
| **TOTAL INCOME – TOTAL COSTS = PROFIT:** | |

## Time spent on

| | |
|---|---|
| Making the work that sold | |
| Accounting (if you do it yourself) | |
| Getting to shows | |
| Setting up and running booth | |
| Packing and shipping online orders | |
| Marketing your work (online or via mailing lists) | |
| Adding new work to an online store and taking down sold pieces | |
| Misc. paperwork (e.g., sourcing materials, show applications, etc. | |
| **Total number of hours spent on business:** | |

| | |
|---|---|
| **PROFIT DIVIDED BY TOTAL HOURS = HOURLY WAGE:** | |

Don't lose sight of your original passion during the financial calculations, though. Hopefully you got into craftwork because you loved working with the medium, and enjoyed designing original work. If the exigencies of making a living from it are turning your passion into drudgery, it's time to consider taking a different job, and pursuing your craft as an avocation. But if you can find that intersection between what you want to make and what the market will buy . . . follow your passion.

Guy Corrie at work. *Photographer: Peggy Parks.*

Stay true to your vision. Be passionate about what you do. If you love what you do, you'll never work another day in your life. That's really important, don't lose sight of that. If you're just in it for the money, well, God bless you, and I'm sure you'll have a great career. But for me, it's about getting up every day and being excited to see what's in the kiln. That was always it for me, and it still is. It hasn't changed.

*Guy Corrie, glassblower*

# CONCLUSION

I hope this book has given you a framework for approaching your craft, both in the design and construction of individual pieces, and in growing your skills and your voice. For those who plan to make craftwork a career, I hope I have given you some ideas that will be helpful on that path.

Producing masterpieces is not magic. Nor does it require inborn talent. To make a masterpiece, you need to have skills, and the willingness to work at developing those skills over time. By looking deeply at the world around you, and evaluating your own work regularly, you'll develop your design and construction skills. By reflecting frequently on your creative process, you'll streamline your methods and find a path that brings you joy.

Go forth and create. I wish you joy, hard work, and success.

*Tien Chiu*

# NOTES

**Chapter 1**
1. Annie Dillard, *The Writing Life* (New York: HarperCollins, 1989), 70.

**Chapter 6**
1. Tim Hurson, *Think Better: An Innovator's Guide to Productive Thinking* (New York: McGraw-Hill, 2008), 71–80.
2. Alex Osborn, *Applied Imagination: Principles and Procedures of Creative Problem-Solving* (New York: Scribner, 1963), 156.
3. Ann Sutton and Diane Sheehan, *Ideas in Weaving* (Loveland, CO: Interweave Press, 1989), 22.

# RECOMMENDED READING

### Books about the creative process

Bayles, David, and Ted Orland. *Art & Fear: Observations on the Perils (and Rewards) of Artmaking.* Eugene, OR: Image Continuum Press, 2001.

Hurson, Tim. *Think Better: An Innovator's Guide to Productive Thinking.* New York: McGraw-Hill, 2008.

Kleon, Austin. *Steal Like an Artist: 10 Things Nobody Told You About Being Creative.* New York: Workman, 2012.

Osborn, Alex F. *Applied Imagination: Principles and Procedures of Creative Thinking.* New York: Charles Scribner's Sons, 1979.

Seelig, Tina L. *InGenius: A Crash Course on Creativity.* New York: Harper-Collins, 2012.

Tharp, Twyla, and Mark Reiter. *The Creative Habit: Learn It and Use It for Life.* New York: Simon & Schuster, 2006.

### Books about visual design

Aimone, Steven. *Design! A Lively Guide to Design Basics for Artists & Craftspeople.* New York: Lark Books, 2007.

Bang, Molly. *Picture This: How Pictures Work.* San Francisco: Chronicle, 2000.

Menz, Deb. *ColorWorks: The Crafter's Guide to Color.* Loveland, CO: Interweave, 2004.

Pentak, Stephen, and David A. Lauer. *Design Basics, Ninth Edition.* Boston: Cengage Learning, 2015.

Wolfrom, Joen. *Adventures in Design: Ultimate Visual Guide, 153 Spectacular Quilts, Activities & Exercises.* Lafayette, CA: C&T Publishing, 2011.

Zelanski, Paul, and Mary Pat Fisher. *Shaping Space: The Dynamics of Three-Dimensional Design, Third Edition.* Belmont, CA: Wadsworth, 2006.

### Resources for creating a successful craft business

Biscopink, Kelly. *2015 Crafter's Market: How to Sell Your Crafts and Make a Living.* Blue Ash, OH: Fons & Porter Books, 2014.

Meltzer, Steve. *Photographing Arts, Crafts, & Collectibles: Take Great Digital Photos for Portfolios, Documentation, or Selling on the Web.* New York: Lark Books, 2007.

Miles, Jason G. and Cinnamon Miles. *Craft Business Power: 15 Days to a Profitable Online Craft Business.* Bonney Lake, WA: Liberty Jane Media, 2015.

Rhee, Mea. "The Hourly Earnings Project." Accessed July 12, 2015. http://www. goodelephant.com/blog/category/the-hourly-earnings-project.

Stanfield, Alyson B. *I'd Rather Be in the Studio!: The Artist's No-Excuse Guide to Self-Promotion.* Golden, CO: Pentas Press, 2008.

Archie Brennan. *Photographer: Susan Martin Maffei.*

## ARCHIE BRENNAN

Archie Brennan began his tapestry career with apprenticeships at Dovecot Studios and Golden Targe Studio, both in Edinburgh, Scotland. In 1963, he became the Artistic Director at Dovecot Studios, creating collaborative tapestries with many British and American artists. As designer and leader of the workshop's weaving staff, he carried out over sixty commissions for public, corporate, and private buildings.

Since 1960, Archie Brennan has participated in more than ninety invitational and juried shows around the world, including over twenty solo exhibitions. His work has been profiled in many magazines, newspapers, and books, and is held in major museums and public/private collections worldwide. He is the subject of three half-hour television documentaries by the BBC, Australia Council, and the Scottish Arts Council.

Brennan has received major art awards from Scotland, England, Lithuania, Switzerland, Poland, Australia, and the United States. In 1981 he was appointed an Officer of the British Empire by Her Majesty Queen Elizabeth II for his contribution to the arts.

Rachel Carren. *Photographer: Elise Winters*

## RACHEL CARREN

Rachel Carren is both an artist and an art historian. She has written extensively about polymer art. Carren wrote the essay on the history of polymer art for Terra Nova, "Polymer Art at the Crossroads," in conjunction with the Racine Art Museum exhibition in 2011; the 2014 catalog for "A Re-Visioning: New Works in Polymer" at the H. F. Johnson Gallery of Carthage College, Kenosha, Wisconsin; and the book *Masters: Polymer Clay*. She is blogmaster of the Polymer Art Archive, an online resource for polymer history, art, and analysis (www.polymerartarchive.com).

Carren's love of textiles and the history of art provide constant inspiration for her own artwork. She has adapted many textile techniques in order to ornament the surfaces of her distinctive polymer jewelry. Her jewelry has won awards and is held in a number of museums. Carren recently developed a method to hand-weave polymer into cloth. This polymer fabric has become a means to explore ideas such as the relationship between clothing and culture.

Rachel Carren. *Divided Sebo Brooches,* 2009. Polymer, acrylic pigment, mica powder. 2.75" × 2.75" × 0.375". *Photographer: Hap Sakwa.*

Carren feels her experience as both an art historian and an artist gives her a distinctive perspective with which to create, consider, and convey the story of polymer. Her studio and writing desk are in adjacent rooms. For more information, visit www.rachelcarren.com.

Guy Corrie. *Courtesy of Guy Corrie. Photographer: Paul J. Smith.*

## GUY CORRIE

Guy Corrie founded his glassblowing company, Union Street Glass, in 1980. He and his wife Leanne began by making one-of-a-kind glass vessels and sculpture, selling at the prestigious American Craft Council shows in San Francisco and Baltimore. In 1983, he exhibited at the Rhinebeck Arts Festival, with remarkable success: over 1,100 hand-blown glass goblets sold at a single show!

Upon returning home, Guy and Leanne hired their first employee and began production. Union Street Glass grew rapidly, selling large orders to the high-end department store Neiman-Marcus, and eventually designing a line of stemware for the chain. The "Manhattan" line, developed for Neiman-Marcus, became the signature line for Union Street Glass, and catapulted them into a new market: tabletop.

From there, Union Street Glass continued to grow. Corrie hired his first sales manager, a business coach, and expanded to twenty employees. It still wasn't enough to keep up with business. The company expanded its market-

ing to New York Gift Show's "Accent on Design," which brought in more wholesale orders. Corrie opened showrooms across the country: New York, Atlanta, Dallas, Los Angeles, and San Francisco. Soon, Union Street Glass had expanded from its humble beginnings in a 750-square-foot studio to a 15,000-square-foot facility with a one-ton glass melter and three 700-pound furnaces, producing and selling 50,000 to 60,000 pieces of hand-crafted stemware and accessories every year.

About Union Street Glass, Corrie says, "Through it all, we never deviated from our original mission: to create contemporary designs using ancient traditions and materials. I think we met those goals and more by creating a body of work that is timeless and will age gracefully."

Guy Corrie. *Sienna Line*, 1996. *Photographer: Geoffrey Nilsen.*

Peter Danko. *Photographer: Tim Rice.*

Peter Danko. *Dresser*, 1997. Birds-eye maple and walnut. 40" × 81" × 18". *Courtesy of Peter Danko. Photographer: Andy Franck.*

# PETER DANKO

Peter Danko is an artist, artisan, designer, and inventor. His designs are in a number of museum collections including MOMA and two Smithsonian museums. His work has been shown in many

college and university galleries. He has been awarded several NEA grants, Best of NeoCon, IDSA awards, and has been awarded many patents, both design and utility. His work is marketed via the A & D design community. Specifiers range from small firms to "starchitects." His designs are used in colleges, corporate offices, churches, synagogues, hotels, hospitals, restaurants, and residences. For more information, visit www.peterdanko.com.

Jane Dunnewold. *Photographer: Jane Dunnewold.*

# JANE DUNNEWOLD

Jane Dunnewold is the former chair of the Surface Design Studio at Southwest School of Art. She teaches and lectures internationally, has mounted numerous one-person exhibitions, and won Best of Show in the exhibition Timeless Meditations (Tubac Art Center, 2013). She has also received the Quilt Japan Prize (2002 Visions exhibition), and Gold Prize at the Taegue (Korea) International Textile Exhibition.

Dunnewold has authored numerous books, including *Complex Cloth* (1996), *Improvisational Screen Printing*

Jane Dunnewold. *Choir*, 2005. Silk, gold leaf, paint, dye. 24" × 72". *Photographer: Jane Dunnewold.*

(2003), and *Finding Your Own Visual Language* (2007). Interweave Press published *Art Cloth: A Guide to Surface Design on Fabric* (2010).

She offers online classes and maintains 1803/Jane Dunnewold Studios in San Antonio, Texas.

About her work, Jane says, "Living creatures contribute to the sacred balance that exists between the seen and unseen; the close-up and the far away. I hope my work—no matter which series I am in the process of creating—will serve as a reminder of the intricate patterns and relationships we miss if we are not paying attention."

Kaffe Fassett. © *Debbie Patterson.*

## KAFFE FASSETT

Kaffe Fassett is renowned for his work with color, especially in textiles. He is the leading designer of needlepoint kits for Ehrman Tapestries of London, designs fabrics for Rowan Patchwork and Quilting, and is the primary knitwear designer for Rowan Yarns. Kaffe has authored or co-authored over fifty books on knitting, quilting, and needlepoint, in addition to his autobiography, *Dreaming in Color.*

Fassett's work has been collected by museums worldwide, and his one-of-a-kind designs have been collected by Barbra Streisand, Lauren Bacall, Shirley Maclaine, and Her Royal Highness Princess Michael of Kent, among many others. In 1988, Kaffe Fassett became the first living textile artist to have a one-man show at the Victoria & Albert Museum. The exhibition was so popular that attendance at the Museum doubled during its run, and it has since visited nine other countries—including Iceland, where 5% of the population attended!

In 2014 the Colour Group of Great Britain awarded Fassett the Turner Medal, honoring him as Britain's greatest colorist.

Kaffe Fassett has been interviewed countless times on national television and radio programs, and was featured in Channel 4's six-part television series *Glorious Color*. In 1999, he presented *A Stitch in Time*, a six-part series for Radio 4. He teaches and lectures worldwide.

About his work, Kaffe says, "Everything I do is about color. My house is a big color laboratory . . . I'm always experimenting and playing to make color as sexy and juicy as I can make it. At the end of the day, I'm trying to get the most out of color."

Norah Gaughan. *Photographer: John Ranta.*

## NORAH GAUGHAN

First published in 1979, Norah Gaughan has been a full-time hand knit designer for over thirty-five years. She once made her living as a freelance designer selling to major yarn companies and knitting magazines, later adding swatch design for ready to wear and a freelance gig on seventh avenue to her resume. She is the author of *Knitting Nature*; *Comfort Knitting*; *Crochet: Afghans, Comfort and Vintage*; and *Knitting and Crochet: Babies*.

Gaughan served as design director at JCA (Reynolds, Artful Yarns, Adrienne Vittadini Hand Knitting Yarns) and more recently at Berroco Inc. where she oversaw the large pattern collection and authored sixteen eponymous booklets. She is now an independent designer collaborating with a variety of entities in the hand-knitting industry, including The Fibre Co. and Loop London. She is also a member of the Brooklyn Tweed design team. Norah's newest book is due out in the fall of 2017.

Norah would like to thank her long-time mentor and friend Margery Winter from whom she learned so very much about the industry and most importantly about pushing boundaries and being creative.

# ANDREA GRAHAM

Andrea Graham is a multi-media artist, working primarily in handmade felt. She incorporates unexpected materials such as branches, glass marbles, and other "found" objects into her organic three-dimensional forms.

Named one of the top influences in contemporary fiber art by the magazine *Fiber Art Now*, Graham has exhibited her work in museums in Canada, the United States, France, and Italy, as well as solo and group shows worldwide. Her work is included in the Sonny Camm collection and in the Claridge Inc. corporate art collection.

Andrea Graham's work has been featured in many publications around the world, including magazines such as *Fiber Art Now, Textile Forum,* and *Filzt Und Zuge Naht.* Her work is featured in the books *500 Felt Objects, 1000 Artisan Textiles,* and *Uniquely Felt,* among many others. She is the recipient of multiple grants from the Ontario Arts Council. Andrea teaches and lectures worldwide.

Ana Lisa Hedstrom. *Photographer: Kim Harrington.*

# ANA LISA HEDSTROM

Ana Lisa Hedstrom's signature shibori textiles are included in the collections of the Cooper Hewitt, The Museum of Art and Design, the De Young Museum, the Oakland Museum,

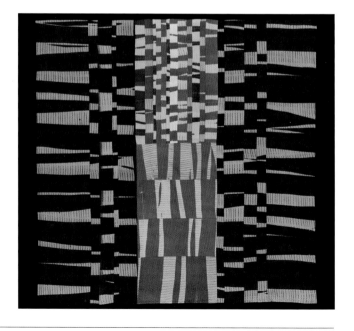

Ana Lisa Hedstrom. *Horizontal Shift.* 43" × 42". *Photographer: Don Tuttle.*

and the Racine Museum. She has completed public art commissions for the City Hall in Emeryville, California, and the American Embassy in Brunei.

Hedstrom's work has been exhibited in Canada, Europe, England, China, Japan, and Thailand. Her teaching engagements include San Francisco State University, California College of the Arts, and numerous international conferences and summer art programs. She has been awarded two NEA grants, and is a Fellow of The American Craft Council.

Paul Marioni.

# PAUL MARIONI

Paul Marioni, one of the founders of the American Studio Glass Movement, started working in stained glass in 1970, started blowing glass in 1972, and developed cast glass in 1978. He has expressed his passion in glass ever since.

Paul's prolific works in stained glass, cast glass, and blown glass (sometimes painted with enamels) have been exhibited widely over the last forty-five years, and have been collected in many museums, including the Smithsonian, the American Crafts Museum, the Corning Glass Museum, and the Museum of Glass. He has completed over 100 public commissions, including cast-glass walls, fountains, skylights, and terrazzo floors.

Paul Marioni has taught widely over the years, at Pilchuck Glass School, Penland School of Crafts, and several universities. He is a Fellow of the American Craft Council, a member of the Artistic Program Advisory Committee at Pilchuck Glass School, and in 2005 received the Lifetime Achievement Award from the Glass Art Society. He has received three fellowships from the National Endowment for the Arts, won the Libensky Award in 2009, and won first prize at the Pacific Northwest Annual at the Belleview Art museum in Washington.

About his work, Paul says, "I work with a difficult medium because I'm a glutton for punishment. Glass is the only material that can capture, manipulate, and magnify light. And light is the most magic of all substances. Glass has that ability to manipulate light. No other material can do it. It's magical. Sometimes it's astounding."

John Marshall.

# JOHN MARSHALL

At the age of seventeen John Marshall ventured forth to Japan for what turned out to be a five-year stint and half-century adventure in historic Japanese textile arts. Apprenticed in traditional doll making, which included weaving, sculpture, and kimono design, John came to specialize in a dye technique that focuses on natural colorants and rice-paste resist techniques called katazome and tsutsugaki.

John has presented exhibitions of his art-to-wear internationally, with shows in Japan sponsored by the US State Department and Kodansha. Today John continues his interest in this art form, lecturing and publishing to ensure that these unique traditional techniques are not lost, while at the same time adapting to a modern and Western environment.

His work has been carried by Julie's Artisans and Bergdorf Goodman in New York, The Textile Museum in Washington, DC, Obiko in San Francisco, and all leading textile galleries in North America, as well as having a thirty-five-year-long association with the Golden Door in Escondito, California.

One of his greatest joys is teaching programs in his 14,000-square-foot studio in rural Northern California where he is able to share the wealth of his library and lifelong collection of rare textiles and limited edition Japanese books.

John's publications have appeared repeatedly in such periodicals as *Ornament, Threads,* and *Surface Design,* and he contributes regularly to *Turkey Red Journal.* His publications in Japan have appeared in *KateiZenka, Shufu-no-Tomo,* and *Sophia* magazines, a whole host of newspapers, and in appearances on NHK broadcasts. Initially publishing through Kodansha International, John currently focuses on desktop publishing of books and DVDs, and writing articles for his blog, helping to spread appreciation and inside understanding of Japanese textiles and culture. For more information, visit www.johnmarshall.to.

John Marshall. *Colors of the Earth*, 1998. Katazome (stencil-applied paste resist) over silk, gold leaf, natural earth pigments. *Modeled by Dr. Helen Petrulio.*

# SUSAN MARTIN MAFFEI

Susan Martin Maffei.

Susan Martin Maffei began her formal studies in tapestry weaving in 1985 with an apprenticeship at Scheuer Tapestry Studio in New York City, followed by a one-year internship at Les Gobelins in Paris.

Maffei has exhibited widely in the United States and abroad, in solo exhibits, group shows, and two-person exhibits with fellow tapestry weaver Archie Brennan. Her work has been collected by several museums, including the San Jose Museum of Quilts and Textiles and the Museum of American Folk Art, and is held in private and public collections worldwide.

Susan Martin Maffei has held fellowships at Australian National University, the Austrlia Victorian Tapestry Workshop, and the New York State Foundation. She has won awards from the National Art Museum of Sport and the New

Susan Martin Maffei. *View up 7th Ave,* 1999. Handwoven tapestry using cotton warp and wool, linen, and silk weft. 30" × 80".
*Photographer: Susan Martin Maffei.*

Jersey Center for the Visual Arts. She has been profiled by *Fiber Art Now* in their series *Fiber Greats,* and by the Textile Study Group of New York.

Maffei has taught workshops and lectures for universities and private groups in Australia, New Zealand, Canada, France, the United Kingdom, Denmark, and the United States. She also teaches from her studio in upstate New York.

About her work, she says, "I search for the marks that relate only to weaving and not to reproduction. I find that understanding is embedded in particular historical Andean weavings, and so of great inspiration in my work."

Debora Mauser. *Photographer: Johnna Goodwin Penrod.*

# DEBORA MAUSER

Debora Mauser attended North Carolina State University, Troutman's, and Leon's Beauty School, and followed her creative passion through the avenue of hairstyling for over fourteen years. Once her son was born, she pursued other creative outlets, and finally landed on making jewelry. It combined her love of personal adornment with the ability to create.

For the last thirteen years Debora has been creating one-of-a-kind jewelry that covers the spectrum of metals, beads, wire, leather and found objects. To satisfy her love of interacting with other like-minded individuals, Debora began teaching her trade over eight years ago. Her teaching has taken her all over the US and exposed her to many techniques and hundreds of students.

Debora Mauser. *Explosion Pendant*, 2015. Copper, brass, and enamel. 3" × 4". *Photographer: Debora Mauser.*

While Debora loves to create, it's the combination of creating, sharing and interaction with students that has truly connected all the elements of her life. Her biggest joy is when the light goes on in a student's eyes . . . the "Aha!" moment. It gives her the knowledge that no matter how small a part she might have, she has ignited a spark in another human being, something to spur them on to create, and find their own voice in their work.

Debora's work follows many paths, and changes and evolves with changes in her life. One unifying theme is texture and movement. She will often layer components to add color and depth, while balancing a piece with negative space so that the focal area is the star.

Tim McCreight.

## TIM MCCREIGHT

Tim McCreight started making jewelry as an Independent Study at the College of Wooster and went on to earn an MFA from Bowling Green State University. He taught metalwork and design for twenty-five years, all the while giving workshops, consulting, and writing books. After writing three books for commercial publishers he started his own company, Brynmorgen Press, which publishes print and digital books, videos, and mobile apps on metalwork and design. Though he primarily works on a small scale, he makes knives, vessels, and tools and has also developed a full graphic design portfolio through books, logos, and websites.

Tim has served on the boards of several local organizations and was on the boards of the Haystack Mountain School of Crafts and the Society of North American Goldsmiths. He was the founding director of the PMC Guild and in that context worked on several international conferences. In 2014 he and Matthieu Cheminée created a philanthropic organization called the Toolbox Initiative to collect tools and materials from jewelers in North America that they give to jewelers in West Africa.

"I think one of the most valuable tools in the arts is curiosity," he says. "I am not so much driven to make beautiful work as simply curious about what might happen when I use a certain tool or combine specific shapes."

Tim McCreight. *Untitled (Brooch)*, 2006. Fine silver. 3" × ¾". *Photographer: Robert Diamante*.

Hiroshi Ogawa.

# HIROSHI OGAWA

Hiroshi Ogawa discovered ceramics his freshman year of college, and instantly fell in love. A few years after graduating, he went to Japan to study Buddhism and pottery, spending time both in a monk's robes and shaping clay at the wheel. Upon his return in 1974, he set up a studio in Carmel Valley, California, and soon built a successful ceramics business, with four or five employees, grossing over $100,000 per year.

In 1981, though, he shut down his ceramics business and moved north to Elkton, Oregon. "I was trying to be creative about what I could sell, rather than what made me happy," he says. "Now I live a lifestyle that doesn't require much money, so I can make the things that I want to make." He built a Japanese wood-fired kiln, christened "HikariGama," and makes one-of-a-kind pieces that he sells in galleries such as Eutectic Gallery in Portland, Oregon.

Because pieces fired in a wood-fired kiln rarely come out the same way twice, he does not try to dictate the outcome. Instead, he partners with the kiln. "One of the problems I've had is that Americans—including me—tend to look at things such as the kiln as a tool. I have never looked at my kiln as a tool. I have looked at it as an entity, one that perhaps has a soul."

In his work, he seeks "shibui," a sense of depth, simplicity, and purity.

Hiroshi Ogawa. *Ichirin Zashi #8.*
Wood-fired clay. 8" × 8" × 16".
*Courtesy of Eutectic Gallery.*

Yvonne Porcella. *Photographer: Luana Rubin.*

# YVONNE PORCELLA

Yvonne Porcella began her career as a textile artist in 1962, making unique garments, wall hangings, and quilts. Her work has been widely exhibited in both solo and group exhibitions. Many museums and collectors have sought out her work, including the Smithsonian American Museum of Art, the Museum of Art and Design, the M. H. de Young Memorial Museum, and the San Jose Museum of Quilts and Textiles.

Yvonne Porcella's work has been featured in over 60 books, including *The 30 Distinguished Quilt Artists of the World, The Quilters Hall of Fame: 42 Masters Who Have Shaped Our Art,* and *Artwear: Fashion and Anti-Fashion.* She has authored eleven books on quilting and wearable art.

Yvonne is the founder of Studio Art Quilt Associates, and served as the President of the Board of Directors from 1989 to 2000. She has also served on the Board of Directors for the San Jose Museum of Quilts and Textiles, the International Quilt Study Center, and the Alliance for American Quilts.

In 1998, she was inducted into the Quilters Hall of Fame in Marion, Indiana, and also became the fifth recipient of the Silver Star Award for Lifetime Achievement at the International Quilt Festival in Houston, Texas.

About her work, she says, "My personal artistic concern is to maintain balance within a unique composition while producing visually pleasurable works . . . My use of bold colors and original designs creates a fresh approach to contemporary art quilts. I use traditional geometric piecing within this milieu and strive for innovation and new perspective."

Yvonne Porcella. *I'm Misty for Red*, 2014. Vintage cotton fabric and Mistyfuse™ fusible webbing. 54" × 50". *Photographer: Cathie I. Hoover.*

Mea Rhee.

# MEA RHEE

Mea Rhee began her ceramics studies in 1994 with a pottery class at a local community center. Pottery quickly became her life's obsession. She established her own studio, Good Elephant Pottery, in 2002, and now sells at prestigious craft shows in the Washington, DC, and Baltimore areas. She also sells in galleries throughout the country. Mea's work has been featured in *Ceramics Monthly, Niche Magazine,* and on Home and Garden Television (HGTV).

In 2010, while deciding whether to quit her "day job" as a freelance graphic designer, Mea started The Hourly Earnings Project, analyzing her pottery studio's costs and sales over an entire year in an effort to determine her hourly income for different types of pottery work. The result? Mea "retired" from graphic design in 2010 and now works full-time at her dream job—throwing, finishing, and glazing pots in her studio.

About her work, Mea says, "I am guided by my Korean heritage, Maryland upbringing, and graphic design education. These things all converge in a style that is simple and natural, but also fitting for a modern world. My first priority for my pieces is functionality. They must perform their intended job, and at a high level, both in terms of design and technical soundness. Every piece is made by hand, one at a time."

Mea Rhee. *Ahjoshi Hanbok*, 2015.
Wheel-thrown stoneware with
porcelain slip brushwork.
6" × 11.5" × 6".

Tommye McClure Scanlin.

## TOMMYE SCANLIN

Tommye McClure Scanlin has been weaving for over thirty years and has explored many different techniques of creating images through the woven structure. In 1988 she left most other weaving methods behind as she began her journey in tapestry weaving. Her tapestries have been exhibited nationally and internationally since 1990.

Scanlin is Professor Emerita, University of North Georgia, where she taught for twenty-eight years and began the weaving program in 1972. In 2015, the Lumpkin County Historical Society presented her with the Madeleine K. Anthony Award for her work with weaving drafts found in the archives of the local library. In 2009 Scanlin was granted a Lifetime Achievement Award for "dedication to craft education" by the Georgia Art Education Association. She also received a Life Membership in Southern Highland Craft Guild in 2009. Scanlin is a Fellow of the Hambidge Center for the Creative Arts and also of the Lillian E. Smith Center.

Tommye Scanlin. *Flight*, 2013.
Handwoven tapestry with soumak.
Wool, cotton, silk. 60" × 52".
© *Tim Barnwell Photography.*

About her work, Scanlin says, "I have to describe myself as both an artist and a teacher. These are the two roles I seem to have chosen in life. Sometimes the balance between the two has weighed more heavily toward one role or the other. However, both enrich my life and I believe each role enhances the other. I'm grateful every day for being able to notice and record parts of the world around me, whether through photos, drawings and paintings, or tapestry weaving. And I find great pleasure in sharing that wonder of the world with others, including ways to creatively respond through tapestry weaving."

Roy Underhill.

# ROY UNDERHILL

Since 1979, Roy Underhill has been captivating audiences in the PBS program *The Woodwright's Shop,* the longest-running woodworking show on television. Roy has a passion for traditional woodworking with hand tools—as he says in one of his books, "How to start with a tree and an axe, and make one thing after another until you have a house and everything in it."

In addition to starring in *The Woodwright's Shop* for over thirty-five years, Underhill has authored nine books—eight classic texts on woodworking with hand tools, and one on communication. In 2015, he published his latest book, *Calvin Cobb: Radio Woodworker!: A Novel with Measured Drawings.* He also spent ten years as the master housewright at Colonial Williamsburg, a recreated colonial town in Virginia, educating the public about traditional carpentry and developing a program at Williamsburg to build houses using colonial tools and methods.

With his show, his books, and his classes at The Woodwright's School in North Carolina, Underhill has instilled a love of hand-tool woodworking in thousands of viewers, readers, and students. His impassioned fans have nicknamed him "St. Roy," which, with typical humor, he attributes to his occasional on-screen mishap in the studio. "I've cut myself so many times on the television program," he said in a 2008 interview with The University of North Carolina Press, "that I remind folks of unfortunate martyrs like St. Sebastian. He met his fate on the receiving end of arrows, and St. Simon has an even more distressing history with the saw. I have the chisel."

About hand-tool woodworking, Roy says, "A big part of the craftsmanship is working in an emergent process. . . . With every stroke of the plane, every cut of the saw, you're responding and building upon the piece. It's like the difference between an acoustic instrument and an electric guitar, or cross-country skiing versus a snowmobile. The feedback between you and the environment is more present and open. You can actually feel the wood and have a dialogue with the material—it's not a one-way conversation."

When not woodworking, Roy enjoys skiing in his money bin, stacking his Nobel prizes in the back yard, and teaching American Sign Language to river otters.

Wayne Wichern. *Photographer: Jason Wells*.

# WAYNE WICHERN

Wayne Wichern's millinery work evolved out of his experiences as a floral designer and a classical ballet dancer, and his interest in fashion and costume design. Wayne grew up on a farm in Cody, Wyoming. His creative career started as a floral designer in Seattle; after some years, he relocated to New York City to pursue dance as a classical ballet dancer. Eventually, after developing an interest in fashion and costume design, he returned to Seattle, where work in theater costuming and retail store and window display transformed into his now thirty-year millinery design and teaching career.

Wayne's elegant hats have sold in such fine stores as Barneys New York and Nordstrom. He has created hats for theater productions of the Belfry Theater in Victoria, British Columbia; Art Club Theater, Vancouver, British Columbia; San Francisco Ballet; Seattle Repertory Theater; and the

A collection of Wayne Wichern's hats. *Photographer: Wayne Wichern.*

Oregon Shakespeare Festival. His innovative hat designs are in collections of the de Young Museum in San Francisco and the Museum of History and Industry in Seattle, Washington. His work has been featured in the *San Francisco Chronicle, Women's Wear Daily, Victoria Magazine,* and *Fiberarts Design Book Six*. Wayne is a skilled teacher who continually works to inspire and encourage students to pursue their interests in professional design careers.

About his work, Wayne says, "Hats are a powerful social and cultural marker. In the early to mid-1900s the daily wearing of hats was a social norm. People rarely ventured out in public without a suitable hat. Today, when you wear a hat you are certain to be noticed. It is always interesting to me to observe the obvious or subtle adjustments of a client's mental and physical attitude as I set a hat on their head. The hat may well ask for a confident straightforward comportment or perhaps a more mysterious or mischievous character is requested of the wearer. Thus the 'theater of the hat,' as each change of hat reveals facets of an individual's persona.

"In continuing traditional millinery techniques I bring together the incredible skills of woodworkers, straw weavers, felters, and flower and feather trim makers into wearable works of art."

Ellen Wieske. *Photographer: Carole Ann Fer.*

## ELLEN WIESKE

Ellen Wieske is co-owner of Dowstudio Showroom, her studio and home she shares with wife and potter Carole Ann Fer on Deer Isle, Maine. She has been a metalsmith and

Ellen Wieske. *Garden Necklace,* 2012. Tin and sterling silver. 20" × 6". *Photographer: Robert Diamante.*

educator for more than twenty-five years. Ellen received her MFA from Cranbrook Academy of Art. She is the Assistant Director at Haystack Mountain School of Crafts.

Ellen has taught at colleges and institutions across the US and France, and her work has been exhibited both nationally and internationally. Her wire work techniques have been documented and published by Lark Books.

## JOEN WOLFROM

Joen Wolfrom.

Joen Wolfrom began quiltmaking in the early 1970s after leaving her career in education to become a homemaker and stay-at-home mom. Her interest in color and design surfaced in the early 1980s. She has taught and lectured in the quilting field, both nationally and internationally, since 1981. Her guest international engagements include working in England, the Republic of Ireland, Northern Ireland, Scotland, Canada, Germany, the Netherlands, Taiwan, Australia, New Zealand, and South Africa.

In the late 1970s Wolfrom began creating commissioned textile art for many private clients and corporations. Her work is included in collections throughout the world. Wolfrom has authored fifteen books and quilt-related products. Several of her books and products have been bestsellers in the art/craft field. Her published works include *Visual Coloring*, *Color Play*, *The Visual Dance*, *The Magical Effects of Color*, *Landscapes & Illusions*, *Adventures in Design*, and *Color Play, Second Edition*. She developed the 3-in-1 Color Tool and the Design Ratio Tool.

Joen Wolfrom. *Pizzazz*, 2003. Quilt sewn from cotton fabrics. 66" × 66". *Photographer: Ken Wagner.*

Joen continues to teach and lecture in the fields of color and design. Loving nature, Joen is now avidly exploring the vast world behind the lens of a camera. Of particular interest to her is both nature photography and experimental photography.

**Tien Chiu** is a nationally recognized, award-winning weaver with more than twenty-five years of experience in fiber arts. She's also a professional project manager specializing in new product development. She applies her insight into industrial methods of designing and building new products, along with her extensive artistic experience, to create textiles.

Chiu teaches workshops on the creative process, writes regularly for *Handwoven* magazine, and is a co-founder of Weavolution, the social network for handweavers. When not weaving or writing, she enjoys adventure travel, making chocolates, and spending time with her husband Mike and two cats, Tigress and Fritz.

She teaches and coaches about the creative process at www.creatingcraft.com, and blogs about her art at www.tienchiu.com.

**Christopher H. Amundsen** is the Executive Director of the American Craft Council.